Seeking Answers Finding Peace:

Loving and Losing Someone with Mental Illness

ENDORSEMENTS

Natalie Ford writes, "When people are hurting, they want to talk to others who have been there. They want to talk to a real person who is not afraid to be transparent." In the wake of the most unimaginable kind of loss, Ford has become such a person. Here she offers the gift of her story, wrapped in compassion for others who grieve. In it you will discover both a friend whose story may help you understand your own, and the true source of all hope.
—**Amy Simpson,** author of *Troubled Minds: Mental Illness and the Church's Mission*

Dr. Natalie Flake Ford brings the dual awareness of both clinician and survivor in her work *Seeking Answers—Finding Peace*. She speaks with raw emotion about her painful journey through her beloved husband's bipolar world and to his untimely death by suicide. This book will offer healing and encouragement to survivors of suicide and shine the much-needed light of hope into the unimaginable darkness loss by suicide engenders.
—**Rita A. Schulte**, LPC, author of *A Roadmap for Suicide Survivors and Those Who Love Them*

In her courageous, uplifting, and informative book, Natalie Ford shares how she survived the death of a loved one by suicide through her deep faith. In addition, she educates with easy- to- understand explanations of bipolar illness, depression, and mental health issues while combining mental illness with God's unfailing love. I highly recommend this compelling book, *Seeking Answers—Finding Peace*, as a guide for navigating the uncharted waters of mental health issues while keeping one's faith intact.
—**Virginia Pillars**, author of *Broken Brain, Fortified Faith*, Mental Health Advocate

Seeking Answers Finding Peace:

Loving and Losing Someone with Mental Illness

Natalie Ford

ELK LAKE PUBLISHING INC

PUBLISHING THE POSITIVE
Plymouth, Massachusetts

COPYRIGHT NOTICE

Identifiers: ISBN-13: 978-1-64949-434-4 (paperback) | 978-1-64949-435-1 (trade paperback) | 978-1-64949-436-8 (e-book)

Key Words: suicide loss, bipolar disorder, survivor of suicide, suicide bereavement, mental illness, faith, relationships

Library of Congress Control Number: 2021949244 Nonfiction

DEDICATION

This book is dedicated to all who have experienced suicide loss. Though the pain is excruciating at times, God can (and in my case did) turn our tears to joy.

TABLE OF CONTENTS

FOREWORD

My relationship with Dr. Natalie Flake Ford began at the height of a crisis she and her husband walked through for years. I'll never forget the day I saw her in the parking lot of our local grocery store. She had urgency and determination in her eyes. She flagged me down and jumped in the passenger seat of my car. Although we'd only recently met, God gave her the courage to trust me that day. She shared with me briefly of her husband's bouts of deep depression. This was shocking to me because I only knew of him as the very tall man who was the life of the party. He made balloon animals, made kids and adults laugh hysterically, and shared the gospel with hundreds of kids in full time resort ministry. Everyone adored Michael and his zest for life. He was a youth leader and his love for God was so evident.

Natalie and I prayed boldly that day in the parking lot. We begged God to intervene and be the help they both needed at that time. We parted ways that day, but our friendship went deeper. We became prayer partners and continued to meet regularly to pray together. Over the years, we would watch God do things that only he could do.

Walking alongside Natalie while she walked alongside her husband, who had a mental illness, taught me so much. I was misguided in my understanding of mental illness and the Christian life. It was in the reading of *Seeking Answers—Finding Peace* I came to an even greater understanding of how to walk alongside a loved one with a mental illness.

Natalie is an excellent teacher, and she knows how to simplify difficult concepts and break them down into practical applications. In her book she tells her story honestly, but she also shares with the intent of helping others who are also on a similar journey.

As a pastor's wife, my husband and I regularly meet with people struggling in life and specifically with mental illness. They have spouses or children who are fighting the battle of mental illness. Some have lost loved ones to suicide, and others live with a fear that one day they will. We have given Natalie's original book, *Tears to Joy*, to many people. It has provided solace and help to each. Ironically one day I in the grocery store parking lot I met a woman while unloading groceries. (What is it with me and grocery store divine appointments?) She told me about losing her son to suicide, and how much she missed him. We talked awhile, and I remembered I had a copy of Natalie's book in my car. I gave it to her. We exchanged names and contact information. The lady messaged me a few days later telling me she read the entire book in one night. It offered her so much hope and comfort. She has since come back to tell me she'll never forget that day in the parking lot and what a gift it was to receive Natalie's book.

If you or a loved one is living life with a mental illness, I strongly believe God has put this book in your hands for a reason. If you feel like you've never been touched by mental illness in your life, thank God loudly. May I lean in and tell you directly chances are you actually are touched by mental illness, you just don't realize it. People are sitting in church pews, preaching from pulpits, sitting in break rooms, and living next door to us who are dealing with mental health issues. Instead of staying silent for fear we might say the wrong thing, we can come alongside them and offer hope and comfort. That's the beauty of *Seeking Answers—Finding Peace*.

—**Melody Hester**, www.melodyhester.com

ACKNOWLEDGMENTS

I'd like to thank my friends and family who encouraged me to rewrite my previous book, *Tears to Joy*. The book you now hold in your hands bears my heart and soul, and I share it with you hoping you will extend grace as you read.

Words cannot express the gratitude I have for the numerous people (I won't begin to name because the list would be extensive) who walked alongside me during times of suffering and of triumph.

Thank you, Susan K. Stewart, for the countless hours you spent editing. I've learned so much about showing versus telling, and I thank you.

Jeff and Jorjanne, I cannot thank you enough for allowing me to share intimate parts of our lives with others in this book. I would not be where I am today without your constant love and support.

Lastly, I want to praise God for the peace that surpasses understanding and unending comfort he has gifted me, and I pray you will experience them as well.

INTRODUCTION

There are stretches in life when we feel as though all our dreams have come true. We are surrounded by people we love. We have great jobs. We adore our spouses. In short, things just couldn't get much better. Then there are times when life throws a vicious curve ball. Nothing makes sense. Everything that once was vibrant and alive becomes desperate and hollow.

In my mid-twenties, I was living the American dream. All of life's best seemed to be coming my way. My husband, Michael, and I were looking forward to growing a family and serving the Lord overseas. I couldn't have asked for more. I had no idea how far we were about to plunge.

Overnight, it seemed, my husband began to experience severe mood swings. He was eventually diagnosed with bipolar disorder. Our lives became a constant roller coaster of highs and lows. Michael descended into severe depression and saw no hope for relief. His agony led him to attempt suicide. Tragically, he did succeed. My heart broke, and I didn't know where to turn. I felt as though God had surely abandoned me; he seemed to answer my cries with silence. My family and friends wanted to help but didn't know how. In short, my fairytale had become a nightmare from which I couldn't wake up.

This book is for those who are hurting and feel alone and hopeless. It is also for those who want to help. Through our struggles with mental illness and suicide, I have learned one thing is certain in life: God is who he says he is. I've realized God is a good God, he is sovereign, and he loves us. This may sound contradictory, but it was this truth that gave me courage to continue when I wondered if I could go on. There were times when I screamed at the Lord in anger and asked, "Why, Lord? Why me?" While I never received a direct answer to my questions, he gave me a far greater gift—his presence.

If you or someone you know is hurting, I pray you, too, will find the hope and peace that only comes from Christ. I want to believe my experience (which is ultimately more about God than about me) will inspire you to cling to the promises of his Word. When you don't understand, seek the face of God. He will give you the strength to weather your own trials with courage and hope.

Exposing my personal loss is painful, but by sharing what happened, I want to undermine the stigma associated with mental illness. Fear of rejection prevents millions from getting the help needed to recover. Research suggests one in four adults suffers from a mental disorder. Truly, mental illness is a disease affecting people from every walk of life. Many of you know someone with a mental disorder. You may be like those of my friends who longed to help but did not know how. This book suggests practical ways you can support loved ones and friends.

Finally, if you're working your way toward recovery, take heart. No matter how bleak you may feel, your disorder does not define who you are. God has a perfect plan for your life.

> For I know the plans that I have for you,' declares the Lord, 'plans for prosperity and not for disaster, to give you a future and a hope. Then you will call upon Me and come and pray to Me, and I will listen to you. And you will seek Me and find Me when you search for Me with all your heart. I will let Myself be found by you,' declares the Lord, 'and I will restore your fortunes and

gather you from all the nations and all the places where I have driven you,' declares the Lord, 'and I will bring you back to the place from where I sent you into exile.'. (Jeremiah 29:11–14, ESV)

CHAPTER ONE

Closing the door behind me, I sighed deeply. I was grateful the doctor said Jorjanne only had a sinus infection. Finally, something simple, something manageable. I tossed my keys on the counter and walked into the bedroom. I noticed the red light blinking on the answering machine and pushed play. Sitting on the edge of the bed, I listened as my husband's troubled voice filled the room.

"Natalie, I just wanted to tell you how much I love you," said Michael. "No matter what happens, I love you. You mean so much to me, and I wish I could be a better husband to you. Tell Jorjanne that her daddy loves her and always will. I love you. Bye."

I stood up from the bed and began pacing as clouds of confusion cluttered my mind. I replayed the message, and tears began to fill my eyes. What was Michael saying? What did his cryptic message mean? Was my husband trying to communicate something deeper?

Was he trying to tell me good-bye?

His depression had been more severe lately, but I hadn't noticed any signs he might be suicidal again. As a matter of fact, he seemed more like himself the past few days. He got out of bed and spent time playing with Jorjanne, and he even rode with me into town to get pizza. Yes, he was definitely better the past few days. His message made no sense.

This morning as I got ready to take Jorjanne to the doctor, Michael told me he was going hiking. He said he needed to spend some time alone with God. I asked him how long he would be gone, and he said until the Lord speaks to me. When I asked what he would do if God was silent, he answered, "Then I guess I'll be gone for a long time." Looking back, I wondered what he meant by his comments.

I crossed the room, grabbed the phone from my nightstand and punched in his number, anxiously waiting as it continued to ring. I shifted my weight from one foot to the other as I cried out to God, "Lord, please let him answer!"

At last, I heard a mumbled, "Hello."

Yes! He answered! I rejoiced inwardly.

"Michael, where are you?" I asked, trying to keep my voice calm.

"I'm in Blairsville. I just left one of the churches here," Michael mumbled. A million questions raced through my mind, but the only ones I could formulate were "Which church? Why are you there?"

"I came to pray. It's one of the churches I spoke at. I can't remember the name of it," Michael said.

"Where are you now?"

"Driving. I'm going into the woods. What did the doctor say about Jorjanne?" He asked, trying to change the subject.

"Sinus infection."

"Let me talk to her," he blurted out with a sigh.

"But I need to talk to you. I have something to ask you." I couldn't imagine why he wanted to talk with Jorjanne.

"No. I need to talk to her. I need to tell her I love her," Michael replied with a hint of desperation in his voice.

"She knows that. First, let's talk." I thought if I could just get him to open up and tell me what he was feeling, I could make it all better. Michael's frustrations were growing as he huffed, "Please put Jorjanne on the phone."

"Okay, I'll put her on the phone, but I want to talk with you when you finish talking to her."

Timidly, four-year-old Jorjanne answered the phone. "Hello."

"Jorjanne, this is Daddy. I just want you to know that I love you. You know that, right? Daddy loves you and will always love you. You are so special to me, and I am very proud of you. Be a good girl and remember I love you." Michael's words were rushed, as if his very life depended on Jorjanne knowing how much he cared.

"Okay, Daddy. I love you too. Here's Mommy."

Snatching the phone from Jorjanne I cried into the phone, "Michael?"

"Yeah?" he answered.

"I don't know how to ask you this, and I really don't want to ask it, but I have to. Are you about to do something stupid?" There. I'd finally done it. I asked him the one question screaming in my mind since I'd heard the message on the answering machine. Shifting my weight and gritting my teeth, I waited for his answer.

"Natalie, I can't take it anymore. I'm so tired of living like this," Michael uttered with a long sigh. "The mood swings are killing me, and I can't be the husband you need. You need more than me. You can do better. I know you'll be okay."

What did he mean? Life had surely been tough, but we'd survived in the past, and we could do it again. Confident I could convince him to come home, I said, "Michael, what I need is you. Please, promise me you won't do anything stupid. Just tell me where you are, and I'll come to you. We can face this together." Unfortunately, he needed time.

"I just need to get away and think. I won't do anything stupid. I just need to hear from God. I don't understand why I can't get over this. I feel so bad."

Pleading with him, I begged him to reconsider.

"Please come home. I love you, Michael. I need you. Jorjanne needs you."

Michael insisted he needed time alone, time to think.

"I love you both. I need to go. I'll call you later."

With that, he hung up. I collapsed on the floor in tears.

Oh, God! What is happening? Protect my husband. Don't let anything happen to him. Give me wisdom. Tell me what to do.

This was not the first time I prayed this prayer. In fact, during the last half of our nine-year marriage, I was accustomed to my husband's extreme mood swings—if such a thing is possible. A year after Michael's normally effervescent personality became erratic and unstable, he was diagnosed with bipolar disorder. We weathered many ups and downs, and over time, his highs and lows had grown more intense.

This was not the first time I feared he would take his own life. Indeed, just months before, he was hospitalized after what seemed to be an intentional overdose of prescription medication.

But he survived.

We survived.

As far as I was concerned, we would again. I only needed to find him and get him to a hospital. Once I found him, he could get help. He could overcome this. He had to—for our sakes.

How could our life together, which began as a fairy tale, become tangled into such a nightmare?

CHAPTER TWO

My wedding day felt magical. All the emotions every young woman feels when she is about to face the man of her dreams at the altar swirled through me. I clearly remember feeling anxious as I stood outside the doors to the church, a bit overwhelmed by the huge step I was about to take. My mom, with tears streaming down her cheeks, whispered into my ear, "I love you." As the doors swept open, I saw my beloved at the front of the church.

My two dads (my dad and my stepdad) escorted me down the aisle. I felt as though I was dreaming. I glanced around me, amazed by the love in the room. My heart smiled as I saw all my friends and family who came to share this special day with me.

It seemed surreal. In moments, I would become Michael's wife. I was only twenty-one and never dreamed I'd walk this path so early in life. I always thought I would be older, with multiple degrees on the wall, before I took this step.

God had other plans, and I was giddy. After this day, my life would be forever changed. God, in his sovereignty, brought Michael and me together. This was truly one of the happiest days of my life.

As the music continued to play, I held my head high and glided to the front of the church to my groom.

It seemed like only yesterday our paths had first crossed. Yes, I knew who he was—everybody knew Michael. We both attended Mercer University in Macon, Georgia. He was Mr. BSU (Baptist Student Union), and I was a RUF (Reformed University Fellowship) girl. I thought he was a cool guy, but we never really talked until one fateful day in the cafeteria. We both walked through the entrance at the same time. He looked at me, then asked, "Where are you sitting?"

My answer was swift and surprised even me. "Wherever you are."

Whoa, Natalie. Slow down. What was I thinking? Being forward was utterly unlike me, but I felt filled with courage when he smiled into my eyes.

We set our books on a table and walked toward the buffet line. Michael smiled at me and asked, "What are you doing this weekend?" My hopes surged. Much to my dismay, my friend, Daryl, walked up as Michael inquired about my weekend.

Overhearing the question, Daryl leaned over and said, "She's going to formal with me."

Oh, no! I was mortified. Michael would surely get the wrong impression, though Daryl and I were only friends. Sure enough, Michael looked at me with those great big eyes, and said, "It's ok. You can sit with Daryl if you'd like. I understand." I assured him I wanted to sit with him, saying, "Oh no. We're just friends. I'd like to sit with you." I couldn't believe I'd just been so bold.

Over lunch, we learned a lot about each other and discovered things in common. We both wanted to go to seminary. In fact, I had just come back from visiting Covenant Seminary in St. Louis, and he was going to visit Southeastern Baptist Theological Seminary the upcoming weekend.

He expressed, "There is another school I'd really like to go and visit, but it is a long drive. I really don't want to drive by myself."

Curious, I asked, "Where?"

"Southwestern Seminary in Texas," he proclaimed. I was shocked to learn he wanted to visit the same school I did.

When I shared with him my desire to visit there he asserted, "Well then, we should go together."

I quickly agreed, although I never expected it to happen.

In just a few short days, Michael began calling the school, arranging for our visit. I couldn't believe we were really going to do this. I knew who Michael was, but I did not "know him, know him." Then came the hard part: telling my parents I wanted to drive cross country with a guy they hadn't met. They decided to come and visit, to meet this man who wanted to drive to Texas with me. My mom and my stepdad drove two-and-a-half hours to meet us for lunch in our college town. As my parents questioned Michael about his hometown, his family and his hopes for the future, my admiration for Michael soared. The conversation was stimulating, and my parents eventually gave their blessing for our trip. In just a few weeks, we began the incredibly long road journey from Georgia to Texas.

To my surprise, this became a life-changing adventure. Michael later told me he knew he would come back from this trip either really liking me or really hating me. Spending so much time together in a car was a great litmus test. It didn't take long for us to realize our commonalities ran deep, and so did our budding affection for each other.

Our visit to the seminary passed swiftly, and on the drive back to Georgia, we began to share our hopes and dreams with each other. The time together launched a season of growing closer, until we began seeing each other exclusively. He embodied many of the qualities I found endearing and crucial to a serious relationship.

Michael would leave me sweet notes on my car; there were mornings when he would drop off a cup of coffee or breakfast with my roommates to give to me when I woke up. We shared picnics both indoors and out. Michael's creativity kept me guessing.

Not only was Michael romantic, but he was also a man of God. Michael's knowledge of the Scriptures and his intimate relationship with the Father impressed me. We spent many nights talking about the Lord, praying together, and reading the Word together. One of my fondest memories was an evening when Michael opened the Scriptures in my apartment on campus and began to share with me about the sacrificial system in the Old Testament. He made Scripture come alive and left me longing for more. I was thrilled to see Michael's love for the Word, and it was this characteristic more than any other that attracted me to him.

As graduation day approached, I found myself on an emotional seesaw. How would I ever live without Michael? We had shared some great times at Mercer, and that chapter of my life was quickly coming to a close. I didn't want college to end, and I certainly wasn't ready to give up my relationship with Michael.

A long-distance relationship never lasted, or so I thought. My mind swirled. *We'll never make it. We'll make promises to each other we can't keep. We'll do our best to make it work, but it won't. It can't.* I found myself both pulling away and drawing closer to Michael.

Had I known what Michael wrote in his journal this same week, I would have been giddy.

> May 29, 1996
> I'm in love! But cannot tell her! I love her more than I can describe. With everything in me, I love her. I wrote her a note telling her this.

He waited an entire month before sharing the note with me.

Again, time was the enemy. I found myself with a kaleidoscope of emotions on the day of graduation. Thinking of the future was thrilling, yet I was terrified. My feelings for Michael were even more troubling. Why was I so upset about leaving him? By leaving Mercer, I was leaving Michael. Why did that bother me so much? Did I love him? Dare I even go there? I'd been ever so careful to guard my heart. Why did it ache so much at thoughts of us parting company?

After graduation, Daddy and my brother agreed to follow me home with a load of my stuff. I went to a graduation party with Michael, then stopped by to tell Daddy I'd be ready soon. I sat in the car with Michael and experienced the greatest heartache I'd ever had in my life.

Finally, I told Michael I would see him later. I cried the entire two-and-a-half-hour trip home, bemoaning the fact I wouldn't see him later. His journal mirrored my feelings.

> June 10, 1996
> I had such a hard time saying 'see ya' not 'good-bye.' I enjoyed Natalie's sweet disposition. When she started crying, I was so upset. I started crying, too.

On the same day, I mailed Michael a letter, which shared my heart.

> June 10, 1996
> Michael,
> Well, I've been home one day, and it's been one of the hardest days ever. The Lord and I have spent a lot of time together. I need him more than ever. I never dreamed it would be so hard—I'm experiencing too much change too fast. The Lord is my Rock, and I'm ever thankful, because I feel as though all of my other stability has been yanked out from under me. I miss you so much already. Everything reminds me of you, and this drives me crazy. I'm counting down the days till I see you again. I feel so cheesy. I've never felt this way before, and maybe I shouldn't be telling you. I don't even know anymore. I rejoice in knowing that God knows.
> Well, I could write you a book and tell you all about my day, but I won't. Suffice it to say I'm learning to trust.

Thanks for being patient with me as I stumble through this letter. My mind is racing with so many things.
Natalie

Two weeks later, Michael came to visit me. We decided to spend the day together at the beach. On the way, Michael distracted me by reaching in the car's console, and a James Avery jewelry store brochure fell between the seats in the car.

"You weren't supposed to see that," he said, grabbing it. A couple of months prior, Michael had told me about a seashell ring he saw at a James Avery store. He went on about how the ring reminded him of me. Had he bought the ring for me? Why was he being so secretive?

When we arrived at the beach, we parked my car and strolled down the beach. We came to a lifeguard chair and couldn't resist the urge to climb up in it. We sat on the chair and gazed at the ocean and at each other.

"Hmmm," I sighed unknowingly.

"What is it?" Michael questioned me.

"I was just reminiscing about a time in middle school when I wrote a song saying how love is like the ocean."

Teasingly, he nudged me, saying, "Well, sing it to me."

Slapping at his arm, I playfully responded, "No way!" He wasn't satisfied.

"Well, if you won't sing it to me, then at least tell me the words."

I thought for a minute before responding. "Love, love is like the ocean. It has its ups and its downs." I stopped. "I can't do this. I feel so silly."

Placing my chin in his hand, he lovingly answered, "No, it's not. Tell me more."

Even though I was afraid to share what was in my heart, I began, "Well, I know love is not about being happy. Love endures the ups and the downs, much like the ocean. When I think of love and marriage, I think of permanence."

Michael reached for my hand and said, "I couldn't agree more. Too many people take marriage lightly. Marriage takes work, but I think it is worth the effort." The conversation had become so intense, neither of us realized hours passed while we sat together in the lifeguard chair.

We climbed down and began walking back to the car. About ten minutes into our stroll, Michael picked up his pace. I was struggling to keep up with him. Before long, he was jogging.

"Slow down," I pleaded. "What's the rush?"

Michael hesitated and finally told me to look at the tide, which had come in considerably. My car! If we didn't hurry, it would be mired in sand on the beach. We raced back. Michael flagged down a Jeep to help us. We hopped in and sped off toward my car.

As we approached my Bonneville, I gasped. There were ten men surrounding my car, trying to push it out of the ocean. I fell on my knees and began to pray as Michael raced to the car. Anxiously, I watched as he climbed into the car, and my heart swelled with relief when I heard the rumble of the engine as it came to life. Five more minutes and my car would have been completely submerged—or worse. It could have been washed out to sea.

Tears were streaming down my face as I cried out to the Lord in thanksgiving. At that moment, I was overcome by the goodness of God. I could not imagine loving him more. God is my protector and my guide, and he loves me deeply. He had blessed my life with an incredible friendship with a man like no other. My heart was so full.

After we washed the undercarriage of the car, we went back to the beach for a picnic. (This time, we parked in the lot—not on the beach.) As we ate our sandwiches, we discussed God's glory. It was truly a time of worship. Finishing up, we decided to take one last stroll. We kicked off our shoes and headed down the sandy beach. Michael seemed distracted; he kept squeezing his water bottle so that water squirted everywhere. Laughing, I said, "Michael, what is wrong with you? You seem so nervous."

Finally, Michael grabbed my hand and said, "Come on. I want to show you something." I followed Michael along the sandy path until we found a spot near the dunes to sit down. Michael continued, "I wrote this for you after our last campus ministry meeting at Mercer. I've waited until now to give it to you. I want you to listen as I read to you."

He read to me:

Natalie,

I have no idea what to say. After this last night of Reformed University Fellowship where I thought I was all cried out, I can't help but cry even more right now. But these tears I shed are tears of joy! I'm in the SGA (Student Government Association) office (hence the stationary), and you're outside sharing the love of God with Amy. Natalie, when you told me you were going to share with this girl, I followed you out the door in order to see where you were going and who you were with. I came to this office to pray. I left this room only to be led to Henry Morris who prayed with me for you. We prayed, and I know the Lord is faithful. He used you, I know. He's using you and will use you in the future.

Natalie, Henry disclosed how he feels about us and said he—Natalie, he told me what I already knew but was too scared to say. I need you, Natalie Pope, to be my helpmate, my soul mate, my best friend, my closest sister in Christ. Natalie, I'm in love with the One who brought us together. Oh, but Natalie, there's more— Natalie, I love you! Wow! These words have never been said about you by me until now. But I cannot fight that God is bringing us together anymore. I love every part of you. I'm scared and will not say this to you until I can follow it up with action. I believe God would have us to be married, but I don't know when.

What was happening here? Tears were streaming down my face. Could it be? I began to shake, not believing my ears. Was he—?

I grabbed Michael in a tight embrace. We cried together. Suddenly, Michael jumped up and began slapping sand fleas off his legs. Laughing, he guided me toward the water so he could rinse off his legs. As the surf rolled over our toes, Michael reached into his pocket and pulled out—what? A James Avery bag? He just told me he loved me, and now he was going to give me a stupid seashell ring?

In what seemed like an eternity, Michael reached inside the velvet bag and pulled out a diamond engagement ring. He dropped to one knee and exclaimed, "Natalie, I love you with all my heart, and I want to spend the rest of my life with you. Will you marry me?

Yes! Yes! A million times—yes! I thought to myself. He picked me up and spun me around as we both squealed in delight.

"Wait," Michael paused. "You still haven't answered me." Grinning from ear to ear, I yelled, "Yes! Yes, Michael Flake. I will marry you!"

Then it happened—that moment in every girl's dreams. The world seemed to stop as Michael gazed into my eyes, cupped my chin in his hands and ever so gently leaned over and kissed me for the first time.

I know by today's standards, to have dated without even kissing sounds improbable and maybe even impossible. We both had regrets from past relationships, though, and were dedicated to the idea of saving those precious moments for just one person—the one God designed to share the rest of our lifetime.

It was worth waiting for.

When our lips finally drew apart, our eyes lifted to the heavens. At that moment, a few days before July 4, fireworks erupted in the sky. Unbelievably, there was also a blue moon.

Perfect! Our long-awaited first kiss ignited fireworks.

Six whirlwind months later, we were married. Michael had accepted a job at Georgia Mountain Resort Ministries in North Georgia, and we began our new life together in the mountains. I soon began working with the youth ministry at Helen First Baptist Church.

We were thrilled with our new home. We spent hours there dreaming and praying about the future.

When it became evident we needed a second vehicle, we began to pray and seek the Lord's help, asking him to help us find one we could afford. We had little money in those days, and the idea of a truck payment was overwhelming. A good friend called us one day and told us he had a Ford Ranger for sale if we were interested.

We drove down to meet him to see the truck. As we took the truck for a spin, it didn't take long for me to realize that Michael loved it. Trying to calm himself, Michael suggested we pray together and ask God for guidance. We prayed and both felt a peace this was the truck for us. The only question was whether our friend would be willing to work out a payment plan.

When we brought the truck back, our friend asked us what we thought about it. Michael said, "Man, I love it! It's great! I only have one question. Will you work with us on a payment plan?"

"Nope," our friend replied. My heart sank. We didn't have any money to pay for the truck up front. Before we could reply, he continued, "My wife and I have prayed about this, and we wanted to make sure you and Natalie liked the truck. If you like it, we will sell it to you for one dollar."

We were stunned.

"No way! Are you for real?" Michael shouted. I stood next to him, speechless, with tears streaming down my face. Our friend and his family grinned as they handed us the keys to our new Ford Ranger. Michael dug into his wallet and proudly pulled out a crisp one-dollar bill.

We were both overwhelmed by God's goodness. It seemed like God was pouring out blessings from heaven into every area of our lives. Not only had he provided for our transportation needs, but he also blessed both the resort ministry and the youth ministry during this time.

In the midst of all of God's favor, our love for each other deepened. Our marriage was an extended honeymoon. Our first anniversary came and went, but I'll never forget the gift Michael gave to me—a James Avery seashell ring.

The more time passed, the more madly in love with each other we became. God was so good to us.

Life with Michael was always adventurous. I had no idea our romance was about to be tested.

CHAPTER THREE

I was surprised when joyful Michael started to become severely depressed. More and more frequently, he felt down and discouraged. Little in life made him smile. Nothing I did seemed to help, and I began to worry about him. Michael, too, was aware of the change.

Michael always thrived on being around people, but something had changed inside him. One afternoon, I walked into the living room where Michael was sitting in the recliner watching television. "Michael, Jim and Angie invited us over for dinner tonight."

He responded, "You go ahead without me. I don't feel like going anywhere."

Frustrated, I urged him, "But, Michael, you haven't been anywhere in days. You sleep and watch TV. It would do you good to get out of the house for a while." I was surprised by his answer.

"No one wants to be around me. I don't really have any friends. Why would anyone want to be my friend? I'm a screw-up. No, I think I'll just stay here."

I was astounded. Michael, the man everyone loved, felt all alone, and nothing I tried helped.

On March 18, 2000, he wrote in his journal:

> I shared with Natalie some of my fears. We had a great devotion on phantoms. I often feel like I have to have everything together all the time. This causes me to be

uptight, and I often shy away from people because I know I am so unraveled. I am scared of questions I cannot answer. I am overcome by fear of the unknown. My faith exercise seems so weak and frail. I often cannot bear the responsibility alone. These words seem so vague and nebulous. I really need to seek the counsel of the Holy Spirit. Do not stop your long-suffering with me. I hate phantoms. They seem to paralyze me, and I cannot seem to break free of their elusive control. Lord, I desire to hear from you more than anything else in the world. Oh Lord, can I hear from you? Speak to me through your Word! Make it clear to me. Help me to see where you are the Creator God, Creator of all good things, even of Natalie and me.

Michael continued to lead the resort ministry, but things were different. He was no longer the enthusiastic, carefree man so many loved. Each day after work, he'd come home and sit in front of the television for hours. Returning phone calls or carrying on a conversation became burdensome to him.

"I feel so empty, so alone," he would tell me. "I feel like I am drowning in an abyss, and there's no way to escape. Nothing I do is good enough. No matter how hard I try, I can't seem to shake the sadness."

My heart hurt to hear such words from a man I loved so dearly. People would tell him to "snap out of it," but it wasn't possible. No matter what we tried, Michael's downward spiral continued. After a couple of months of despondency, Michael finally went to our family doctor, who prescribed an antidepressant. Still, the depression continued to linger, taking Michael down a path of despair.

Michael had little energy. He'd always loved the outdoors and would jump at the chance to go camping or hiking. His best friend, Chad, called and left a message on the voicemail inviting Michael to go hiking. Even this was not enough to motivate Michael to leave the recliner. No matter how much I pushed, he refused to even return Chad's call.

"It's just too much effort to talk to anyone right now," he said.

"But Michael, this is Chad we're talking about. You love to go hiking with him. Why don't you give him a call?" I suggested. He continued to rest in the recliner, making no move for the phone.

Michael didn't want anyone to know about the depression. He was embarrassed. The fact he didn't want anyone to know about his struggle left me feeling very alone. I felt helpless and didn't know where to turn. I couldn't share my concerns with anyone else, so I kept my private anxieties to myself. I, too, began to feel sad and isolated as I wrestled with changes with no support.

One sleepless night, Michael wrote:

> I feel so depressed. I don't believe I've ever felt as down in the dumps as I've felt for the past two and a half months. Oh, Lord, if only I could hear from you, and if only you would show me your plan for my life. What I am putting Natalie through is not fair in the slightest. I seem to be forgetting so much of the things that used to make me the happiest. As I pen this entry, I am sitting next to a beautiful waterfall in the Chattahoochee National Forest. My thoughts seem to be colliding into one another. Oh Lord, if only I could have one clear thought and even act out upon it. I would be so much better off.

We felt like we were falling deeper and deeper into a cavern, and we didn't know how to stop. Michael wanted to spend most of his days in bed but forced himself to get up and go to work. When the summer missionaries arrived to work with the ministry, it took everything Michael had to supervise them. In the past, Michael found great delight in getting to know that the staff. But this year, it was like everything else—incapable of bringing him out of the pit.

The summer missionaries had never met the vivacious, full-of-life man I fell in love with. They only knew a man who appeared wounded and scattered. Some began voicing their concerns with me.

"Is Michael OK? We don't really see as much of him as we thought we would." I didn't know how to respond because I didn't want to betray Michael's trust. It was important to him to maintain his image of having it all together. Usually, I'd answer the missionaries and others with "He's just not feeling very well."

Summers were always insanely busy for us. Not only did the resort ministry race full speed ahead, but I also took the youth at church to camp. As the time for me to leave for camp drew near, Michael became more and more apprehensive about being alone.

"Do you have to go?" he asked.

Uncertain what to do, I replied, "Do you want me to stay home?" Scratching his head, shifting his weight he replied, "No. You need to do your job. Go ahead." We'd been apart on numerous occasions. Where was this insecurity coming from? As I continued to pack, I noticed the tears.

"Michael, are you sure you will be OK with me gone?" He wiped away the tears with the back of his hand.

"Yeah, I'm sorry. I'll be fine." I didn't know what to think or do. I felt pulled between my role as a wife and as a minister.

The day I left Michael was a wreck. He had dark circles under his eyes and hadn't showered in several days. He moped around aimlessly and wept continually. I felt trapped between my responsibility to the church and my devotion to my husband. I decided to be dutiful in my job, so I hit the road camp bound. As I got closer and closer to our destination, fear began to overtake me. I'd never seen Michael so depressed and so hopeless.

"Don't go, Natalie. I can't bear the thought of being alone. I feel so scared," Michael had said. "I don't know what I am doing anymore. I feel like I am drowning, and I wish you didn't have to go."

"Lord, am I doing the right thing?" I asked. When I arrived at the conference center, I saw my friend Doug Couch and immediately began to cry. Placing his hand on my shoulder, Doug asked, "Natalie, are you OK?" As much as I tried to hold it in, the tears fell.

"Not really. I'm worried about Michael. He's going through a rough time, and I'm not sure I should be here at camp or at home with him. He's very depressed, and I have to admit I'm scared for him."

Frowning, Doug asked me, "Do you think Michael might hurt himself?" I hadn't really thought about it. Now I really was afraid. Honestly, I didn't know what to expect. Reluctantly, I answered, "I really don't know."

Doug reached out and hugged me saying, "Natalie, go home to Michael. We can take care of things here."

I called to tell Michael I was back home, and he responded, "I can't believe you came back." When Michael walked in the door, we raced into each other's arms. We clung to each other like our lives depended on that moment. When Michael was able to regain his composure to speak, he asked, "Why did you come back?" Looking at him through the tears, I said, "I had to come back. Michael, I am worried about you. I think we need to get some help." He agreed. "You're right. I can't continue to live like this."

It took a few weeks to get an appointment with the doctor, and Michael's depression worsened daily. I've never been so scared and felt so out of control. I wrote in my journal:

> Dark, dismal days. I've never been so afraid in all my life. Michael has been struggling with anxiety and depression for the last six months. I can't remember the last time he slept through the night. Tonight, he took a prescription sleeping pill and two Tylenol PM. He's groggy, and his vision is doubled. He mutters to me. I'm not sure whether this is just giving him rest, or if he needs to go to the hospital. Did he take too

much? Has he overdosed? What should I do? This is such a lonely place to be. Lord, grant me wisdom. I know this spirit of fear is not from you. Give me peace. Heal Michael. Lead us to the right counselor. Give him rest, physically and emotionally.

Lord, without you, I'd lose my mind. I hate pretending all is fine when inside I am crumbling. At times I feel I must even hide from Michael so I can be strong for him but so often my tears give me away. I love him as I've never loved before, and the thought of losing him tears me apart. Father, please heal my love. Give us the comfort that only comes from above. Thank you for ministering to my soul in worship last night. Thank you for assuring me of your constant presence. You will never leave me nor forsake me. Be real to Michael. O Healer, free his pain. Help me to be a support to him. Take away my moments of weakness when I want to lash out. May I scream at the sickness and not at you or Michael.

Even though I don't understand at all, thank you. I sing of how I long for brokenness, and you have answered that prayer. For so long, I believed I had to be strong, but no—when I am weak, you are strong. I am right where you want me. Teach me to be content. I love you, Lord!

Journaling my prayers was therapeutic for me. It helped me to process the hurts I had been holding inside. One of the biggest mistakes we made was keeping our struggles a secret; this fueled our shame and increased the burden we felt to fix things. We were missionaries after all; we were serving God. If we couldn't pull it together what message would that send to others? We believed these lies. Sometimes I wonder how our story might have changed if we'd been honest with those we loved sooner.

CHAPTER FOUR

A month later, Michael's mood dramatically improved. His joyous spirit was restored, as well as his zest for life. We were ecstatic about the changes in him. We were happy the depression was gone, and our lives could return to normal. I can't express how relieved I was to have my husband back.

Unfortunately, our joy was short-lived. Michael's mood changed dramatically causing our lives to feel topsy-turvy. Michael was no longer depressed, nor was he acting like himself. He was easily agitated, manipulative, controlling, and, at times, downright mean. Not the man I married. I didn't even like this man. I wrote in my journal:

> I'll never forget sitting in Henry's office in his home for our premarital counseling. One of the questions he asked us will stay with me always. He asked Michael and me why we loved each other. We began to list all of the reasons why. He then asked if we woke up one morning, and everything we loved about the other was gone, would we still love one another? That day, I quickly answered, "Yes!" (without fully knowing the implications). Even today, I am just beginning to understand.

> The last six months have been the hardest of my life. Michael's depression was controlling our lives. At times, he was even suicidal. I never knew from one moment to the next who my husband would be. After months of praying for deliverance, we finally sought medical help.

Our doctor diagnosed Michael with General Anxiety Disorder (GAD) and put him on medication. After a month without change, the dosage was increased and almost immediately Michael became an obnoxious beast. Who was this man in my husband's body? Surely, he isn't the same man I married.

When the depression subsided, super-hyperactivity set in. His moods were now manic. Michael still didn't sleep, no longer due to nightmares, now due to excessive energy levels. As he went without sleep, he constantly kept waking me up deeming six hours of rest was laziness, and I needed to get up. Without notice, he removed himself from his meds, which threw him into an abyss of hatred and rudeness. Never had I seen Michael behave so poorly, both to me and others. I found myself constantly embarrassed and often apologizing for him. The tears seemed to fall endlessly.

I didn't want Michael in the pit of despair, but I didn't like his new, out-of-control personality either. I felt like a yo-yo, being bounced up and down with his ever-changing moods. The worst part—Michael didn't see it.

"I feel better than I have in years. I don't know why everyone wants me to go back to the doctor." Trying to get him to understand he was not well was so frustrating.

"But Michael, you are not well. You run around like a chicken with your head cut off and accomplish very little. You're always on edge, and it's driving everyone else crazy." No matter what I said, he couldn't understand.

$$\diamond \diamond \diamond$$

For months, Michael and I had been planning a vacation. We were both excited about the trip because we needed a break from the craziness of summer. Since the depression had lifted, Michael was convinced all was well. But it wasn't. As it got closer to time for our vacation,

Michael became busier and busier. The summer staff had gone home, and the busy schedule was winding down with the resort ministry. But it was as if someone had wound Michael up like a top and set him loose.

Before the sun would rise, Michael would leave for work. We were still sharing an office at the church, and I would come in to find the office a disaster after cleaning it the day before. We would put in our hours, and I'd go home, but Michael always found more to do. What was amazing was he was so busy—yet he was accomplishing so little. He often stayed at work until after midnight. If I took a day off or left work early, he'd call wanting me to join him on some excursion.

"Natalie, what are you doing? Let's go to the park and have a picnic," he'd say. Two hours later, he would call again.

"Natalie, it's gorgeous outside. What do you say we go for a walk?" As nice as a walk might have been, I had work to do, and so did he.

"Michael, I can't. I'm working." Before I could even refocus, the phone would ring again.

"If you don't want to go for a walk, how about we go visiting? There are lots of people we haven't seen lately." Michael seemed to have lost all concept of time, and work was no longer a priority. Three days passed without Michael taking a shower, and he called our friends and bragged about this. He was proud he had so much energy.

Finally, the day came for our departure. I had packed all our bags so we could leave that morning. I awoke to find a note that said, "Be back shortly." I got dressed, loaded the car, and waited for Michael to return. I waited. And waited. And waited. No Michael. At noon, I began to call him. After several tries, I finally reached him on the phone. He was ecstatic.

"Natalie, you'll never believe what I found out!" he gushed. "Ground school is going on this week. I called and I can take classes toward my solo pilot's license!"

"What about our vacation?" I questioned.

He exclaimed, "We're still going. I'll just drive to Atlanta every afternoon for class, and I'll be back at night. We'll have the mornings together."

Michael's decision infuriated me. I had been looking forward to this trip for months. Surely, he wouldn't leave me on vacation in the mountains alone.

Would he?

We drove to the mountains and unpacked. The whole time, I was hoping he'd given up on the whole flight school idea. After dinner, I put in a movie by Gary Smalley about marriage. Michael announced, "Good. I'm glad you chose that one. Enjoy it while I'm gone."

He was seriously going to flight school. This vacation was about us, and he wanted me to work on our marriage alone while he drove all the way to Atlanta and back. I was livid. After he left, I wept like never before. The tears seemed endless. What was becoming of our marriage? We had been so close—best friends. I didn't even know who Michael was anymore. I was afraid. Would the man I knew and loved ever be the same again?

Michael didn't see anything wrong with the arrangement. He left about 3:30 each afternoon and drove to Atlanta, returning about 11:00 each night. He woke up early every morning to study his lessons for flight school. We'd go to the river or the pool for a couple of hours, then he was off again.

I did a lot of thinking in those lonely hours. My prayer was for the Lord to daily increase my commitment to Michael and allow me to cherish our vows. It was not an easy prayer, but I was sincere and kept praying it. Somehow, we survived the week and returned home.

✧✧✧

This cycle of desperate highs and lows continued. Our doctor suggested Michael see a therapist, so we began meeting with a Christian counselor who gave us many practical suggestions to help with the depression. While the counselor was helping, it still wasn't enough.

We eventually began to look for a psychiatrist. Entering this new territory was terrifying, but the results were astounding. The doctor explained to us Michael was experiencing mania. He explained this often caused hyperactivity and increased anxiety. He prescribed a new regimen of drugs, and Michael's mood and his attitude slowly improved. Initially, the doctor did not tell Michael his diagnosis. Michael was depressed and knew he needed medicine to help. The doctor believed telling Michael he had bipolar disorder could increase his negative thinking and suicidal ideation, and so we decided to wait to explain to him. Michael became more amiable. With the help of our counselor, we were finally able to talk through some of our issues. Healing began in both of our lives and in our marriage.

After the doctor told me Michael's formal diagnosis, I began to research bipolar disorder. I learned the reasons for Michael's changed behavior. Like others with bipolar disorder, he experienced moods that are higher than normal, mimicking the highs of a person on drugs. I hadn't realized he enjoyed the highs and used words such as "feeling alive, energized, closer to God, and able to conquer the world" to describe it. My experiences were the high clouded Michael's judgment and increased risky behaviors.

We felt we could beat bipolar disorder. This was new territory for us, but not for the doctor and the counselor. They helped us navigate the changing waters, and we felt optimistic about the future.

CHAPTER FIVE

Advances in modern medicine have made treatment options for bipolar disorder more readily available. Michael was taking his medication and seeking counseling; we were hopeful.

Still dreaming of serving together on the international mission field, we moved to Louisville, Kentucky, to attend seminary. The day before we left North Georgia, we found out we were having a baby. I was ecstatic! Surely our lives were turning around. Michael was doing well. We were pursuing our dreams, and now we were expanding our family.

As classes began, I found myself absolutely in love with the academic community. Michael, on the other hand, was miserable. He was having a difficult time making friends and had become antisocial again. There were days when I couldn't get Michael out of bed to go to class. This was especially challenging because we had all our classes together. The professors always asked me where Michael was, and I didn't know how to answer. How should I tell them, "He didn't come to class because he's feeling sorry for himself, and he's really down?" Instead, I'd give the standard, "He's not feeling so good," and I eventually began to believe this myself.

Other days, Michael cried for hours. This was a difficult time for us. I was pregnant, which meant both Michael and I were on a roller coaster ride of emotions. I felt like I was always trying to pull him up.

We started seeing another counselor, and he looked Michael squarely in the eye, and said, "Your erratic behavior patterns appear to be attributed to your bipolar disorder." Michael's jaw dropped.

"What? I don't have bipolar disorder," Michael demanded. "No one has ever told me this before. Where did you get such a crazy notion?" Michael retorted. Michael had been diagnosed with depression, but no one used the word "bipolar" until now.

The doctor continued, "Michael, I'm sorry no one told you, but it is in your records. You need to acknowledge you have a mental illness. You have bipolar disorder." This news devastated Michael. He denied the possibility for weeks.

"Natalie, you don't believe what the doctor said, do you? Tell me you don't think I'm crazy," he would plead. I'd answer as calmly as I could muster.

"No, Michael, I don't think you are crazy, but we have to admit you haven't been yourself for some time now. Maybe we should consider the possibility the doctor is right." He was embarrassed and ashamed. Because I had researched the disorder, I was convinced this was a legitimate diagnosis.

Acknowledging my husband had a mental illness was challenging; it was something that happened to other people, not to us. Because Michael loved God and was trying to please God, he thought he was somehow immune to such negativities. We learned no one is immune.

As we progressed in our schoolwork, Michael's misery deepened. We realized both of us continuing to go to school once our baby was born would be difficult. We began to pray and seek the Lord.

Despair seemed to define Michael during those days. He hated the cold, snowy days. He hated the city life. He longed for the mountains. He began to dream of moving back to North Georgia to start our family. I had my doubts. The church sent us off to seminary with the understanding we'd become international missionaries. What would everyone think if we packed up and came home after one semester?

When our pastor called, Michael shared his desire to return. I was pleasantly surprised when Pastor Jim assured Michael saying, "We love you. I know the church would welcome you back with open arms. You are going through a difficult time, and you need support. Let us be that support for you." His encouragement was a relief and answer to prayer. We returned to Georgia, and Michael resumed the job he'd left behind.

I wish I could say everything got better. It didn't; things got worse. While Michael responded well to the cocktail of medications prescribed by his psychiatrist, every time he became symptom-free, he would stop taking the pills. This threw us back into the cycle of manic and depressive episodes.

About a month after we got back, Georgia Mountain Resort Ministries hosted a carnival downtown. By then, I was eight months pregnant. Because I couldn't stand the scorching heat for long, I worked at the hospitality center for our volunteers. Michael showed up late in the afternoon and asked, "Hey, will you ride with me to the church to pick up some more balloon animals and water bottles?"

Reluctantly, I agreed. "OK, I'll go."

All the way to the church, Michael berated me. "You don't care about my ministry, do you? Why did you even come? Why aren't you outside working?"

I tried to explain. "Michael, I'm eight months pregnant, and it's ninety degrees outside. I'm working at the hospitality room inside." He wasn't satisfied.

He yelled, "Well, the least you could have done was bring me something cold to drink while you sit inside enjoying the air conditioner, knowing your husband is dying of heat. And what about lunch? You didn't bring me any lunch, either!"

On and on he went. *Who did he think he was?* By the time we got to the church, I was furious. I lit into him. "Michael, that's enough! I'm sick and tired of you yelling at me. You are mean and manipulative. You need to change your attitude, or you're going to end up running this carnival alone. Do you know how many people have come into the hospitality center complaining about your behavior?" Maybe it was not the right way to respond, but I was furious.

He looked at me with hatred in his eyes, and said, "You are a sorry excuse for a wife. If you cared about me at all, you would be outside working beside me all day. I don't know why I put up with you!"

He began cussing at me, and I looked at him and said, "I'm not going to take this. I'm leaving." As I turned to walk out of the church, he grabbed me and threw me over his shoulder. I began kicking and screaming.

"Put me down! You're going to hurt the baby! Stop it! Quit!" On and on, I pleaded with him to put me down. I was terrified. I was so afraid he was going to hurt the baby. I thought about yelling for help, but no one else was in the church.

I'm not sure what got through to him, but he finally threw me off his shoulder and sat me in a chair, where he held his hands firmly on my shoulders, making sure I couldn't go anywhere. He got right in my face and began to sob.

"I am so sorry," he said. "I should have never said that. I'm hot. I'm tired, and I've got to get back to work. We'll talk more later." That was the end of the discussion. He drove me back to the concessions area where I stayed the remainder of the day with a lot on my mind.

How dare he treat me that way! How could the gracious, compassionate, loving man I married have turned into such a monster? I wrestled with this question and more in the weeks that followed.

By the time August rolled around, the medication had finally taken effect (it generally takes six-to-eight weeks for antidepressants to reduce symptoms), and Michael's mood began to stabilize. We both began to prepare for the birth of our precious little girl with eager anticipation.

On August 28, 2001, Rebekah Jorjanne Frances Flake was born. Michael was so supportive that day. He was thrilled to be a new dad. We both thanked God for blessing us with the joy of a little one.

The first couple of months after we brought our daughter home were special. Michael and I grew closer as we discovered the joys of parenting. We would stand beside Jorjanne's bed and watch her sleep. Michael would lie on the floor beside her and try and make her smile. We floated in a continuous state of awe that God had given us such a precious gift.

CHAPTER SIX

I truly believed having a baby would turn things around for us. I thought Michael would recognize his importance as a parent, and the responsibility would be enough to keep him accountable for his recovery. Unfortunately, I was wrong. We continued to walk through an abyss of highs and lows as he failed to comply with taking his medications. In the beginning of his illness, Michael was depressed about twice a year. As time passed, he became depressed three to four times a year and was manic just as often. As he began to accept this diagnosis, he journaled:

April 17, 2003

Well, it all seems to boil down to the quality-of-life issue. Do I want to continue on with the massive cycles from extreme highs to extreme lows? I am going through the wringer of emotions again. Kathy [our counselor] says that I am chronic. I have a chronic disease. I am bipolar. If it had been forty years ago, I'd be in and out of hospitals, but now I have medicine, and for me not to take it means I'm throwing away the gift God is giving me. I really need to get more focused and stay focused. Lord, please help me. My thoughts run as rapid as the stream behind me here at Panther Creek. If only they could run in the same direction as the stream and not everywhere. I've got to leave this place and get some work done. Oh Lord, where is my passion for life? Where is it? Help me, Lord, to trust in you. My words seem so meaningless right now. Please put meaning back in my words, Oh Lord!

What words can I put on this page or on any page that could really express the total sadness in my heart? I have lost my passion for life and for living. Constantly I struggle with sad thoughts and feelings of hopelessness. Where, O God, are you? Where is the passion I once had? Am I just living a life of confusion? I lack the clarity of thought to make wise decisions. What is it that clogs my ears so I cannot even hear your still, small voice? Why, O God, must I suffer with this living hell? Where are you when I call out to you?

O God, surely there is more to life. I feel like such a hypocrite. Why do I have no joy and a cloud of doubt that hangs heavy around my spirit? Where are you in my life? Why is this my lot? Oh God, please free me from this awful depression! I feel safest in bed all curled up. Why are my thoughts so jumbled? Why must Natalie endure this again? Where is my positive attitude and my joy for living? Where are you, oh Lord? Why am I so dead?

Eventually, Michael went back to the doctor, and his medications were adjusted again. Michael was still having a hard time accepting that he needed medications. Michael told me, "Natalie, I keep hearing voices in my head telling me the doctor doesn't really care about me. If he did, he wouldn't charge such exorbitant fees." Michael knew these voices were lying to him, but he still heard them, and, at times, he listened. Taking medicine was a constant battle for Michael. Once again, he abandoned his medication, and the depression returned. I learned this is a pattern with individuals with bipolar disorder, and some say it is a symptom of the disorder itself.

Each time Michael would stop taking his medication, I would become infuriated with him. Why couldn't he just take the stupid medicine? After all, it was helping him. Every time he came off the meds, he put us back on the roller coaster. I was at the end of my rope and didn't know where to turn for help. In desperation, I wrote:

> My heart hurts like never before. My daughter looks at me with compassion and says, "Are you sad, Mommy?" How should I respond? I'm dying! My husband treats me like a slave—if I question him or fail to do his every wish, I am told I no longer care about our marriage. I was yelled at for throwing away the packaging for chicken, Cool Whip, and strawberries. He yells at me for cleaning; he yells because I don't clean. Lord, what am I to do? I'm in a no-win situation. There is no peace in my life right now. I'm living in turmoil. Please help his medicine to work! I can't continue to live like this.

> What am I to do? I am committed to this marriage, but I refuse to be treated with such continual disrespect. Should Jorjanne and I leave for a while? If so, where do we go? She needs stability and consistency, and I can't provide either when Michael is so unpredictable.

> Earlier this week, Michael hung my pajamas all over the house and put his clothes in my drawer. When I asked him about this, he walked around, grabbing my pajamas from the house, and began throwing them into the trash. I tried to talk with him, but he refused to listen. To my knowledge—my pajamas are gone, much like my dignity.

> My love language is quality time, but that is impossible right now. When I have time alone with Michael, he tells me all I am doing wrong, and I don't care. I am standing beside him because I do care! Father, I don't know what to do or not do. Perhaps the hardest thing is knowing we may have this "thorn" for the rest of our lives.

> Draw Michael unto yourself. Make him a man after your own heart. Help him to see his mania. Give him the desire to change. Protect Jorjanne. Guard her eyes from this. Help her not to see her daddy in a bad light. Help me to trust. Lord, be my strength, my Rock, and my Fortress. I need the comfort found in the safety of your arms. Hold me and give me peace.

Michael's mania continued to escalate. He spent several nights at the office because he had "so much work to do." He'd come home and shower—on a good day—and leave again. From what I could tell, he wasn't accomplishing much in his hours at work. People began calling our house looking for him because he had failed to return their phone calls. I made excuses for him and tried to cover as best I could. I cried every day for two months. I feared I'd never smile again.

Summer was quickly approaching, numerous volunteers would soon be coming to North Georgia, and Michael was responsible for scheduling their assignments. He asked me to help him make out a schedule for the summer. Before I could get out of bed, he left with Jorjanne to go hiking, so I got up and worked on some schoolwork.

He came home and began shouting, "Why aren't you working on the schedule? I thought we agreed when I left you were going to work on the schedule?" Shocked, I shouted back.

"Michael, you've been hiking. You didn't seriously expect me to do your job for you while you were out playing, did you? We can work on it together now that you are home."

Michael responded by yelling, "You don't care about me or my job. I don't need your help!" He stormed out of the house and began working in the yard.

After some time, I cautiously approached him and asked, "Do you want to work in the yard, or do you want my help with scheduling?" I should have stayed out of his way.

"I told you I don't need your help! You don't care about me, so just leave me alone!" he screamed.

Jorjanne and I loaded into the van to get away for a while. I just needed some space. I was putting the car in reverse when he picked up the doghouse and set it behind the van so I couldn't leave. He climbed into the backseat of the van and proceeded to yell at me. After much shouting from both of us, Jorjanne looked at Michael and said, "Daddy, get out of this car and go."

Oh, how my heart broke. Our little girl was seeing all of this. What had become of us? Michael angrily burst out of the car, and I drove to a friend's house so I could clear my head. Several hours later, we returned home to find Michael asleep in the backyard.

I felt like the pain would never end. Every winter, Michael sank into the abyss. In the summer, he soared into space. When would it end? Again, I poured out my heart in my journal:

> May 9, 2004
>
> Lord, you know what has happened, and you know what it will take to bring healing. I hurt like I've never hurt in my life. I keep thinking there are no more tears to cry, but here they come again. Will they ever stop? Will I know happiness again this side of heaven? I need to be strong for Jorjanne's sake. She needs stability, and nothing seems stable in our home anymore. Life is chaotic. Give me the peace that surpasses understanding.
>
> I know your plans are greater than what we can imagine; help me to live in light of this truth. I can't carry this burden alone. First and foremost, I need you. Secondly, I need the Body of Christ to help strengthen me each day. I've never felt so alone in all my life. I'm desperate for you, Lord! Please carry me through!

A month passed, but the mania did not. Michael and I went to a counseling session, where we talked about finances. Michael had been on several spending sprees, and money was tight. The session went well, and we ventured to Walmart afterward to pick up a few necessities. As we were walking inside, Michael said, "We are going to buy a tree together today and plant it as a reminder of this day as a financial milestone in our marriage." He began to point out all the different trees, asking me if I liked any of them. I was frustrated because we'd just spent an hour talking with a counselor about how little money we had.

Finally, I spoke up and said, "Michael, I don't want a plant. We need to save our money." I turned and began to walk off when he hollered, "Natalie, stop! Come here. Don't walk ahead of me." He was treating me like a child. I bit my tongue, turned and walked back to him. He picked up a twenty-dollar Christmas tree and put it into the buggy.

I said to him, "I really don't think we need another tree."

That did it. He lit into me and began swearing at me. Never had I heard such talk come out of his mouth. A lady looking at plants nearby glanced our way and began backing away. I said, "Michael, I'll wait for you in the car." He followed me to the car and berated me all the way.

"You are so selfish! It's always about you. I want to buy a tree to symbolize the new life for our marriage. But no, you don't care. You never care!"

I clammed up. He screamed and cussed because I wasn't talking to him. Embarrassed and angry, I mumbled back, "Michael, I can't talk to you when you are like this." He yelled, "You never talk to me! You don't care about our marriage." His words hurt more than he would ever know. It was love—not the emotion, but the verb—that kept us together.

Later that night, I wrote in my journal:

> Lord, I know he is unwell, and I know we are all sinners. How do I respond? I'm so tired of this mess. It would be so easy to just give up. Do I get some space between us for a while? Do I allow myself to be spoken to with such disdain and disrespect? Help me, Lord. I want to show Christ's agape love to him, but it's so hard. I never dreamed I'd be in a marriage where I was treated like trash. He even told me, "I wouldn't treat you like a dog if you didn't act like one." Ouch!

> Father, I know our marriage isn't pleasing to you. It must either disgust you or break your heart. Heal our marriage. Heal our hurts. Help me to be a woman pleasing to you. Hold my tongue. Help me to watch

Michael fall if that's what it takes and help me to do so without nagging him. Help!

I'd never felt so desperate in all my life. I had to cling to God as if my life depended on it, and in many ways it did. While our circumstances didn't change instantly, my attitude began to change. The more I prayed, the more I read the Scriptures, the more peace I felt. God heard my cries. He had not abandoned me.

CHAPTER SEVEN

As time progressed, so did Michael's mental illness. I could no longer cover for him at work. His attitude with his staff was unacceptable, and his supervisors called him in for a meeting. When asked how he was doing, Michael readily admitted things had gotten off to a rocky start. His supervisors told him he needed to get help, and they were granting him a leave of absence from work. He would be out of work for the duration of the summer.

Reluctantly, Michael agreed to visit the psychiatrist—mainly to appease his employers. A few days later, we met with the psychiatrist, and Michael was visibly antsy. He had a difficult time sitting still. His thoughts were bouncing from topic to topic.

The doctor asked Michael, "Have you had any thoughts of hurting yourself in the past?"

"Yes," Michael answered.

"Have you had any of those thoughts recently?" the doctor continued.

Michael paused, looked at the floor and whispered, "Yes, I have." The doctor explained to Michael he needed to go to a hospital.

"At the hospital, you will receive better treatment. They will be able to monitor your medications and help you get the disorder under control. What do you think?" There was a long silence. Finally, Michael mumbled, "OK."

The doctor offered to call an ambulance, but without really thinking about it, I said, "I'll drive him."

His nerves really got the best of him as we drove to the hospital.

"Natalie, I am so scared. I don't really need any more help. I'll be OK. Let's just go home," he pleaded. "I promise I will take my medications, and everything will be better." I wished I could believe him, but I knew if I didn't take him to the hospital now, he would never go.

"Michael, the doctor thinks the hospital is the best place for you now. We need to go." My head ached, and so did my heart as he begged me not to go.

"Please, please. I am begging you, Natalie. Don't make me go there. I'll do anything. Just please don't make me go to the hospital."

As we pulled into the parking lot, Michael began vomiting. He was more nervous than I'd ever seen him. He sat in the car and refused to get out. He began to sob uncontrollably. I kept coaxing him and pleading with him, and after thirty minutes in the parking lot, he reluctantly agreed to go inside with me.

Once inside, Michael was escorted into a separate room for a psychological evaluation. I sat in the waiting room, praying this would help him. After what seemed like forever, a staff member came and took me into the room with Michael.

"Mrs. Flake, the doctor signed a 10-13, which means Michael has to stay here until a psychiatrist releases him." I glanced over at Michael, and he was livid. He sat with his arms crossed and gritted his teeth. He shot daggers at me with his eyes.

As soon as the counselor left the room, he lit into me.

"You knew it! You don't care about me! You just want me locked up and out of your life. You and the doctor conspired against me!" After a cascade of accusations, he told me to leave. "Go! Get out of here! I don't want you here, and I don't care if I ever see you again! You are a liar. You and the doctor connived and planned a way to lock me away. I hate you!" I fell into a chair and began to sob.

"Michael, that's not true. I love you. I just want you to get help. Your job is on the line. You desperately need help. We need help." I cried. He gave me the silent treatment. He refused to even look at me while I sat with him for another half hour in total silence.

The intake specialist returned and said to Michael, "It's time to take you to your room. Mrs. Flake, you are welcome to walk with us so you can see where Michael will be staying." We walked down a long, cold hallway, through multiple locked doors, and finally entered the wing where Michael would stay.

The first person we saw was a man in his mid-twenties who had suffered a head injury and had wires coming out of his head. The next man who walked by was mumbling obscenities under his breath. Michael turned to me and pleaded, "Please don't leave me here." My heart was breaking. We were given a tour of the ward, then we had a few minutes alone before I had to leave. Michael began crying, begging me not to leave him in this place. Walking away from him that moment was one of the hardest things I have ever done.

As the escort unlocked the door and closed it behind us, I was startled by a loud thump. I turned to see a man being wrestled to the ground and put in restraints. Trembling, I asked, "What just happened?"

The specialist explained, "The man you saw was trying to escape. They will sedate him and put him in isolation for the disturbance." I fell apart before I even made it to my car. I cried until there were no more tears to cry. Would Michael be OK here? Did we do the right thing? My heart was aching, and I was so fearful for him. Broken and weak, I drove home to take care of our daughter.

When Sunday rolled around, I knew I needed to go to church, but I wasn't sure if I could handle it, so I did what every "good" Christian does. I put on a good front, and I went. I smiled on the outside, while inside I was crumbling. Two friends knew what was going on, as did our pastor. I could hardly look them in the eye for fear I would start crying. I sat in the back, and as soon as the service ended, I darted out the door.

I talked to Michael on the phone every night. The first conversation was heated. Michael was still furious with me for "sending" him to the hospital. In time, the anger subsided, and he began to admit he had a real problem.

The following weekend was Family Weekend at the hospital. My parents kept Jorjanne so I could go to the hospital and take classes about mental illness. At the workshop, I met other family members who were trying to help their loved ones cope with mental illness.

I came to recognize I had become codependent. I thought by covering up for Michael (returning phone calls for him, answering emails, going to his office after dark) I was helping him. I learned I was enabling him to continue down a destructive path. I was preventing him from facing the consequences of his actions. I realized, as hard as it would be to watch, he needed to fall so he could rise.

I went to some classes by myself and to others with Michael. We attended group therapy and were able to sit down together with the doctor and talk about our own circumstances. This time was beneficial to us as individuals and as well as a couple. Throughout the weekend, Michael came to the realization he was thankful he was getting help. He also recognized he was not "crazy" or "stupid," but he was a normal guy who had an illness. We met doctors, lawyers, professors, and other professionals who struggled with bipolar disorder. Connecting with others helped Michael to understand this illness doesn't discriminate and helped tear down some of the stigma we carried regarding bipolar disorder. Meeting professionals who were both intelligent and successful normalized the illness for Michael. He no longer viewed it as a "weak person's disease" but realized the disorder was no respecter of persons. When the weekend was over, I returned home, and a few days later, I was able to go and bring Michael home.

During the time of his hospitalization, I had to explain to Jorjanne why her daddy wasn't home. Michael traveled a good deal for work, I said, "Jorjanne, daddy is out of town for a few days. We are going to have some fun mother/ daughter time together." She didn't question me; she responded, "OK, mama. Sounds good." Anyone who called received the same answer. While we were coming to terms with the illness, we were still not ready to be open about it with others. Michael resumed work in the fall and his mood improved—for a time.

After a few months of relative calm, the rapid cycling resurfaced. Michael's anger escalated over the holidays. We were visiting my mom for Christmas. I loaded Jorjanne into the car as my mom climbed into the driver's seat. I clicked the car seat's safety belts into place around Jorjanne and was walking around to the passenger side of the car when Michael came running out of the house toward us. "Where are you going?"

"We are going to town to run a few errands," I responded.

"Why are you taking Jorjanne? She can stay here with me," he yelled as he yanked open the car door nearest Jorjanne.

"No. I'd rather she come with me," I replied, feeling Michael's mood was too erratic to leave her alone with him.

"She's my daughter, and she is staying with me," he screamed.

My mom was stunned, and quietly turned around to look Michael in the eye and said, "Michael, please let her come with us. I don't get to see her very often, and I'd love to spend time with my granddaughter."

Unmoved by her plea, he retorted, "She is my daughter. You lost your Jorjanne (my sister who passed away as a child), and you can't have mine!" When he said these words, I couldn't hold back my anger any longer. I screamed back, "Get away from this car! We are going to town, and I don't want to see you when we get back. You need help, and I will not let you speak to us this way."

Later the same day, Michael returned home to Cleveland, Georgia, without us. My parents were afraid for me and encouraged me to stay with them until Michael's mania subsided. I needed a break, or I was going to have my own mental breakdown. We spent most of the month of January apart from each other.

During this separation, Michael went to many of our friends and told them I was leaving him.

"I think Natalie is leaving me. I don't understand why, but she has moved in with her parents."

Friends began calling me, asking, "Why are you leaving Michael? He loves you. You need to come home. Y'all could go to counseling."

They were unaware of Michael's illness. Some would advise me saying, "Natalie, you can't live like this. You deserve better. You need to leave Michael." Others would caution, "Divorce is wrong. You committed to him in sickness and in health."

I had no intention of divorcing Michael; I only needed some space before I lost my mind and ended up in a mental health facility myself. I wanted to protect Michael, so I didn't tell most of the people who called about his illness. I would respond, "Things are complicated, and I'll return home when the time is right."

The more calls that came, the angrier I became at Michael. I felt like he was making me the bad person. Being away for so long was hard, but it was harder when I had to lie about why I was away.

I finally said, "Michael, I am done with the lies. I will not cover for you anymore. I cannot pretend everything is okay when it isn't." I felt like I was drowning with no chance of rescue. I wanted his blessing to tell others about his illness. He did not want me to tell anyone what was going on.

"Natalie, you can't tell anyone. What would they think? I am a minister. I am supposed to have it all together. We can't tell people." He still didn't understand. I tried to explain.

"Michael, I need support. I'm going to lose my sanity if I can't share with one or two people, we both trust. I need a safe place to be real." The realization began to dawn on him, and he hesitantly agreed.

"OK, you can share with someone, but we both need to agree on who to tell." We discussed "safe" people in our lives, and once we began to tell a few close friends, I began to feel I could breathe again.

I learned the power in sharing my pain with others. When I brought the truth of Michael's illness out of the darkness and into the light, I found freedom and liberty from the shame that had forced me into isolation; it is no surprise the Scriptures call us to carry one another's burdens because in doing so, the weight of suffering decreases.

At the end of January, Jorjanne and I returned home. Michael was beginning to come down from the mania, and healing began in our marriage. We continued to go to counseling, and we tried hard to communicate with each other. Michael had a renewed passion for his ministry and was seeking restoration with many of the people he had hurt. Hope seemed a possibility in our lives.

CHAPTER EIGHT

In early spring, we were hosting a Resort Ministry Conference to train and equip leaders who would be bringing teams to the North Georgia area to work. Michael invited other resort missionaries from the Southeast to come and speak at the different sessions. The ministry was once again thriving. I was proud of Michael. For some reason, he didn't share in my excitement. He was terrified of the conference being a flop. "What am I doing?" he would say. The closer it got to the conference, the more I felt Michael pulling back. His attitude became negative, and his self-confidence all but disappeared.

The day before the conference, Michael told me he needed some time alone to get ready for the event. He'd not been sleeping well for weeks; he saw the doctor and got a prescription to help him rest. I went to the resort ministry office to work on some final details for the event and was gone all morning. After lunch, I tried to call Michael, but he didn't answer. I assumed he was sleeping. I continued working. About 3:00 p.m., I decided to stop and go exercise. As I was driving to the gym, I felt an overwhelming sense of panic, as though God told me to go home. I tried to shrug off the feeling, but I keep hearing this pervasive voice in my mind telling me to go home.

Reluctantly, I made a U-turn and went home. I walked in the door and called for Michael. There was no answer.

I went into our bedroom and found Michael sleeping soundly. I went over to wake him, but he didn't move. I shook him and called out his name. Still, he didn't move. At first, I thought he was playing around with me. I shook him again. Panic threatened to overtake my voice when he didn't respond. Had he taken the sleeping pills the doctor had given to him? I was furious with him for not waking up.

"Michael, wake up! This is not funny. Get out of bed!" I walked around the bed, placed both hands on his shoulders, and began to shake him. He didn't respond. Not sure what to do, I called our friend Jim and told him what was happening.

"Jim, I think I should call 911. What do you think?"

Without hesitating, Jim said, "Yes, make the call."

As I called 911, I walked into the bathroom, searching for clues. I saw the bottle of sleeping pills on the counter and picked it up. Oh God, no! The bottle was empty, and it had only been filled a couple of days earlier.

I stayed on the phone with the dispatcher while the ambulance was en route. When they got to the house, the paramedics grabbed Michael by the shoulders and sat him up; they began shaking him trying to wake him. I fought back the sobs as I prayed silently. After what seemed like an eternity, Michael muttered unintelligible sounds, and they gave him something to make him throw up the medicine in his system. Before long, he went from being incoherent to vomiting yellow stuff all over our bed. My heart was racing. I began pacing the floor, wondering what in the world I should do. A million thoughts soared through my mind. *Would Michael recover? Would I survive his overdose? I should not have gone to work. I should have left earlier. Were there warning signs I missed? Who do I need to call? Should I pack him a bag? Would I be able to sleep in our bed again or would I always remember the moment I couldn't wake him?* On and on my mind raced.

Before the EMTs left, Jim was at my house. As we followed the ambulance to the hospital, Jim called Michael's mom and my parents for me. The doctors gave Michael charcoal to help eject the contaminants in his system. Our former pastor and friend, Kyle, and his wife, Alanna, were on their way to the Resort Ministry Conference, so we called and told them what happened, asking them to come to the hospital. I paced the parking lot looking for them. I couldn't sit still. My heart was racing; my head was pounding, and I had to keep moving to stay sane. When I finally saw Kyle and Alanna, I ran to them, and I collapsed in Alanna's arms. After a few minutes, I encouraged Alanna to go to the church to work on conference details, while Kyle waited with us at the hospital to find out Michael's prognosis.

I'll never forget Kyle holding a pan for Michael while he vomited charcoal everywhere. It was a disturbing but selfless picture of true friendship.

After several hours, an intake specialist from the mental health department came and evaluated Michael.

He told us, "Mr. Flake is going to have to go to a psychiatric hospital tonight." Michael was still nonresponsive. I asked, "Will you please call his doctor and see if we can get him into the hospital where he went before?" Unfortunately, it had no openings, so Michael was admitted to a local facility.

As I prepared to leave, I realized the conference was scheduled for the next day. I couldn't possibly deal with the conference tomorrow. No way I could face everyone in light of what had just happened. I began to panic. Kyle lovingly hugged me and said, "I'll take care of tomorrow. You go home and get some rest." All I could think about was what we would tell people about Michael. I couldn't tell them he overdosed. He would be humiliated. What should we do? After much deliberation on my part, I decided it was best to tell people he was in the hospital due to a reaction to some medication.

It's the truth, right? I told myself.

It was early morning by the time I got home. After a restless night, I got up with an emotional aching in my chest. Because of the conference, Jorjanne was spending the weekend with my parents, a blessing. She had not been home to see any of this. However, the house was deathly quiet that morning, and I hurt.

After Michael's first night at the psychiatric hospital, I went to visit. Michael hugged me over and over, saying, "I wasn't trying to take my life, Natalie. You must believe me. I was just so exhausted I needed sleep. No matter what I tried, I couldn't rest, so I decided to do whatever it took to get sleep. I took two pills and was still awake. An hour later, I took more. Honestly, I don't remember how many I took." I was skeptical, but I so desperately wanted to believe he was telling the truth. We never discussed it again.

While I was there, I asked to speak to a doctor. No one at the hospital would talk to me. I frantically paced the halls searching for someone—anyone—to give me answers. It was against their regulations to discuss a patient's treatment with family. I felt like this was just an excuse not to talk with me. Michael had previously asked the doctor to call me, but he refused. Michael had no idea how long he would be there. I needed to know when to pick him up. Despite having a signed release of information giving doctors permission to talk with me they refused. We both felt helpless.

In the meantime, I called Michael's psychiatrist. "Michael is in the hospital, and I'd like for him to be transferred to Ridgeview, so he is under your care."

The doctor replied, "As soon as a bed opens up, I will make sure Michael is moved."

On my birthday, Michael came home from the hospital. We had decided upon his release he would voluntarily check himself into another treatment facility for more long-term care. We had one day together before he would leave again.

We spent the day together in superficial conversation. We talked about the beautiful weather. We discussed our daughter. He apologized for ruining my birthday celebration. I lied and said, "All is well." Honestly, I just wanted the day to end, so I wouldn't have to face the pain of disappointment. Neither of us discussed what had occurred. It was as though we wanted to pretend his overdose had never happened.

The next morning, I drove Michael to the psychiatric hospital where he would stay for several months. I visited on the weekend for another family workshop, and I met with his doctor and attended seminars to learn even more about bipolar disorder. Finally, Michael transferred to the day program, and he spent his days in treatment, but was able to leave at night. We did this for several more weeks.

While Michael was away, life was tough at home. I was constantly afraid of the phone calls. Youth pastors would call inquiring about bringing a team to work with us, and I made excuses for why Michael was away. Friends, who were unaware of his illness, would call, and I felt like it would be disrespectful to share with them that he was at a psychiatric hospital.

I lived in constant fear of his boss calling to fire him. Though he had been off work for several months, they continued to send his paycheck. My house felt as though it was built on sand, and it was shifting day by day. Never had I felt so alone. God was my only strength and refuge.

Five months later, Michael was finally released from the hospital's care. He still had regular doctor visits but no longer had to go to the hospital daily. He seemed more himself than he had in years. I felt as though I had my husband back. We spent time together; we played together. He and Jorjanne spent lots of time playing hide and seek, pretending to blast-off, and just plain old wrestling. Life was beginning to look up. I was cautiously optimistic. After years of searching, I finally found my husband again. The Lord restored his joy, and his moods stabilized.

Michael was learning to recognize the warning signs of his illness and was doing a better job at managing the symptoms. He wrote in his journal:

> These pages are turning faster and faster as the years go by. I feel like I am in a really good place now. I've enjoyed this for about sixteen weeks. I've been looking for triggers and have noticed a few major ones. Additional stress, for one. Not just the kind that comes from daily living, but also the kind that comes during the holidays. Forgetting my quiet time with the Lord does not help at all. Thank you, Lord, for helping me.

Now that Michael recognized his triggers, he had to face the challenge of overcoming them. The first real test came as we faced the first holiday since his road to recovery had begun. Wednesday morning, we left to celebrate Thanksgiving with family. We found out when we arrived my aunt had been diagnosed with lung cancer. Everyone was nervous about this—everyone except for Michael.

I was amazed at his ability to calm a stressful situation. He even stayed up late, talking with my aunt, encouraging her to trust the Lord of the storm. I was so proud of Michael that weekend. This was a crucial moment in my heart. For the first time in years, I was beginning to respect and admire my husband again.

We survived Thanksgiving without a hitch, and I began to remember all the reasons I fell in love with Michael. It had been four months since he experienced any bipolar symptoms. We began putting the broken pieces of our marriage back together. I found myself truly enjoying my husband's company.

A couple of days after Thanksgiving, we took Amtrak cross-country—from Atlanta to Reno—for a conference. We spent a lot of quality time in cramped quarters. We talked and even dreamed of our future. We watched movies on the train and shared our deepest thoughts with each other. We had a layover in Washington, DC, so we decided to do a little sightseeing. Hand-in-hand, we traversed DC. We talked about travelling together as a family. We discussed what it would be like to raise a teenager. We considered what our lives would look like as we aged, and what we would do after retirement. We were both happier than we'd been in a long time; we were falling in love all over again.

We eventually made it to the conference. Reconnecting with old friends was a blessing for both of us. Michael was able to spend a substantial amount of time at the conference with our friend, David.

David had heard about Michael's overdose, and so he just asked him straight out what was going on. At first, Michael tried to divert the questions. After thirty minutes of avoidance, he began to open up. For the first time, Michael was honest about his struggles. He told David about the illness, the medications, his resistance to taking the medicines, and his fears. I was proud of Michael. This was a real breakthrough for him. He was finally accepting his illness and was beginning to have the courage to face it.

CHAPTER NINE

December came into our lives as a sweet kiss on a cold winter morning. Michael dimmed the lights and played Christmas carols on the CD player as the three of us decorated our Christmas tree. Michael put Jorjanne on his shoulders and let her hang ornaments near the top of the tree. Giggling, she clung to his neck. At times, Jorjanne would lean down and kiss the top of Michael's head. Turning off all the lights, Michael put the angel on the top of the tree. He then offered up a prayer for our family. As he said, "Amen," he turned the lights on the tree so the moment we opened our eyes, we saw everything glowing and cheerful. It was magical! Michael leaned over and kissed me, assuring me we had been offered a new start. We were so blessed.

Filled with happiness and joy, I took a group of students from church to Passion, a conference for college students. For the first time in a long while, I was able to worship the Lord with gladness and praise in my heart. God had not only restored my marriage, but he had also restored my joy.

In one of the first sessions, John Piper spoke about the reality of suffering. "Suffering exists to display the greatness of the glory of God's grace." He continued, "If you are a missionary, you should expect hardship because the only way others see how satisfied we are in Christ is through suffering."

Was that what God had been doing in our lives? I listened to him and prayed God would use the turmoil of the past four years for his glory—even as I felt relief the worst was behind me.

Later, as I looked at the list of breakout sessions, one stood out to me. It was entitled, "When Life Hurts," led by Francis Chan. In his talk, Chan spoke about times in his own life when God didn't make sense. As I listened to him share, I felt the weight of all I had experienced. Still, I was praising God for delivering us from it.

Amid my praise, Chan asked the crowd, "How many of you want to be like Jesus?" Hands shot up all over the room. Of course, we wanted to be like Jesus. Next, he asked, "How would you respond if God told you the only way to make you more like Jesus was to bring suffering into your life?"

Now wait a minute, I thought. *My life has been a living hell. The last thing I want is to face more suffering.* In that moment, the Holy Spirit spoke to me and said, "But don't you want to be more like Jesus?" Immediately, my heart cried out, "Yes, Lord, but ..."

I don't remember much else about the session. At that moment, the Lord began carving away at my will. I left the session and kept hearing Chan's question resounding in my mind: "What if the only way for you to become more like Jesus is through suffering?"

I began wrestling with the Lord. *NO! I don't want more suffering! Haven't we had enough?* When I went into the next seminar, the adults were encouraged to find a place in the room to be still before the Lord. I sat for what seemed like an eternity and wept. God's words, "If you love me, you will obey me," came into my thoughts. What was God trying to tell me? I'd been trying to obey him. After all, I was a missionary. I'd given up my life for him.

Next, the Holy Spirit spoke to my heart with words that pierced the very depths of my soul.

"Do you trust me?"

Of course, I do.

"No, Natalie. Do you trust me?"

Things began to come into focus for me. If I truly trusted God, I would surrender to his will, even if that entailed more suffering. Could I do that? Did I really trust God enough to surrender to suffering? I wept and wrestled with God—until, at last, I gave up.

I prayed to the Lord the hardest prayer I'd ever uttered: *Lord, I want to trust you. My spirit is so weak. Forgive my unbelief and give me the faith to trust you. Even if it means more suffering will come into my life, I ask you to make me more like you.* I got down on my face before God and cried until the leaders asked us to leave the room.

I went outside to call and tell Michael about my encounter with God. The moment he answered the phone, I knew it had returned. I could hear the depression in his voice. NO!

"Michael, are you depressed again?" I asked.

Through the tears, he sighed and answered, "I wanted to surprise you. I quit taking all my medications at Thanksgiving. I was feeling so much better, I really believed God healed me. I wanted you to see how well I was doing without the medicine. Only I'm not doing well. I'm worse."

I returned home to a very melancholy husband. He'd spend all day in bed. When a good friend called to check on Michael, I told him the depression had returned. We called the psychiatrist, and Michael resumed taking his medications. Every day for two weeks, our friend came over in the morning to pray with Michael and encourage him to get out of bed. As soon as his friend would leave, Michael would either crawl back into bed or move to the couch.

As frustrated as I was with Michael for coming off his medications, I also had a strange peace. I knew that God was with me. Ever since my encounter with God at Passion, I knew God had not forsaken us. He was molding us into his image, refining us in the fire.

A couple of weeks later, the college ministry and I shared with the church the lessons learned at Passion. For the first time, I told them about the encounter I'd had with God as a result of Francis Chan's talk. "I felt like I was in a wrestling match with God. I'm so tired of hurting, but I really do want to be more like Jesus." I said, "My life has been hell the last few years, and I don't know what tomorrow holds. I don't want things to get bad again, but what I do know is no matter what happens, God will be with me." No one really understood the significance of my statement. As best they could, the people in church that night encouraged me and promised to pray. I went home feeling very loved.

I truly meant every word I said. I was not facing this life alone. God was with me.

Five days later, I found the frightening message from Michael on my answering machine.

At the time, I truly thought Michael was getting better. The week started with a small victory. Michael went with me to pick up dinner. This was huge. It was the first time he'd been out of the house in two weeks. I went to bed thinking we'd made progress. Michael had not only gone with us to get pizza, but afterward, he went to visit a friend. I thought perhaps his depression was finally going to disappear.

He spent a lot of time playing with Jorjanne. I watched him laugh with her. He smiled as he watched her giggle. He read books to her. He tickled her. He seemed to be enjoying life again—until the following morning

Then I hit play on the message machine.

"Natalie, I just wanted to tell you how much I love you." said Michael. "No matter what happens, I love you. You mean so much to me, and I wish I could be a better husband to you. Tell Jorjanne her daddy loves her and always will. I love you. Bye."

I felt as though my world was spinning. When I had left the house that morning, he told me he was going hiking. He wanted to spend some time alone with the Lord. I thought it was a good sign.

What was this ominous message all about? Overcome with emotion, I called our friend who had been visiting Michael every day.

"Mr. Bob, I'm not really sure what's going on. I got a message on the answering machine from Michael, and I have this gnawing fear he was trying to tell me goodbye. I'm afraid he's going to try and hurt himself."

Mr. Bob thought for a minute and asked, "Do you want me to call the police so they can look for him?"

We agreed this was the best option. If we could just get Michael home, then we could take him to a hospital to get help.

Time continued to tick by with no word from Michael. I was getting more nervous. Where was he? Why hadn't the police found him? I prayed and prayed for him during those long hours. Throughout the day, I repeatedly called his cell phone, to no avail. Around 6:00 p.m., he finally answered.

"Michael, I'm so glad you answered. Where are you?" I began. He sounded frightened.

"I'm not sure." He sounded so confused. This was so unlike him. He knew these mountains like the back of his hand.

"Where did you park?" I asked, searching for any clues to help us locate him.

"I don't remember," he replied.

Getting desperate, I asked, "Well, at least tell me what you can see.?"

He was quiet for a few seconds and answered, "I can see Mt. Yonah." Michael sounded like a frightened child. "Natalie, I can't keep living this way. I'm so tired of the constant mood swings. I am so scared. What if I never get better? I can't go on like this. I won't keep doing this to our family. I keep hearing voices telling me to end my life. I am so scared." It was the end of January, and the temperature was dropping. Michael was shivering as we talked.

"Do you have a jacket and gloves? It's getting really cold outside," I questioned him.

"No, I don't have any food either, and I'm getting hungry," he answered. I was shaking too now, but not from the cold. Never had I been so afraid.

"How about a flashlight; surely you have that?" I asked.

"No, Natalie. I don't have a flashlight either."

I pleaded with him. "Michael, please start walking down the mountain before it gets any darker. There are people looking for you. Please, listen for them. I need you to come home. We can face this together. I need you."

Michael's cries were ripping at my heart.

"I'll try, Natalie, but I am so scared. I love you. I really do, Natalie. I'll always love you."

Tears were streaming down my face. "I love you too, Michael. Come home to me, baby."

Shortly after I hung up the phone, there was a knock at the door. I opened it to find a police officer ready to write a report.

As we spoke, he kept asking, "Are you sure your husband isn't playing some sort of joke? Are you sure you didn't misunderstand? Maybe he is out hiking or camping."

I was furious he would suggest such a thing.

"Michael is not playing a joke. He is in danger," I cried. "You have got to find him before it's too late!"

I told him what little information I had gotten from Michael about his whereabouts, and he said, "Well, ma'am, we haven't even found his truck yet. We'll continue to look for him, but if we don't find his truck soon, we'll have to call off the search."

Call off the search? Michael was out there cold and alone, terrified of both life and death, and they might call off the search? I refused to let my mind dwell on the possibility. I begged the officer to do what he could.

Once again, I found myself on my knees. Not long after the officer left, Jim, the friend who drove me to the hospital when Michael overdosed, and Doug, Michael's boss, came to the house. They told me of their concerns and sat with me as we waited. And waited. And waited. My mom continued to care for Jorjanne and put her to bed for me.

And we waited.

About nine o'clock, the search party found Michael's truck. I was so relieved. I called Michael's doctor to tell him about the day. He reserved a bed at the psychiatric hospital for Michael that night. I told the officers when they found him, I wanted him taken directly to the hospital, and I would meet them there.

I anxiously awaited their call. Jim and Doug were still waiting with me, and I tried to convince them to go home. "They'll find Michael, and he'll go to the hospital. There's really no reason for you to stay." They both insisted on remaining with me.

We prayed and made small talk as we all anxiously awaited news. Minutes turned into hours. At midnight, still no word. About 1:00 a.m., I finally called the police station to see what I could learn. They told me someone was on the way to my house to talk with me. About 2:00 a.m., a car drove up. Jim went out into the yard to meet him, and I stood, wringing my hands nervously. I opened the door, and to my horror, there stood a man in a cleric's collar.

Without hearing a word uttered from his mouth, I furiously cried out, "No!"

The priest looked at me and said, "I am so sorry. Michael's gone."

Tell me this is a nightmare! Someone, please wake me up! I screamed inwardly. Michael can't be gone. What will I do without him? What about Jorjanne? His mom? My mind was racing. On my knees with tears streaming down my face, I began to drill the minister with questions about the night.

We all cried and held each other for what seemed like an eternity. Then it struck me. I had to tell Jane. Michael's mom didn't know. I had called her earlier in the day, and she was waiting at home to hear from me. I wracked my brain, trying to think of someone who lived near her who could go to her. The only contacts I had in Atlanta where she lived were unwilling to tell her about Michael's death, and so it came down to a decision: either the police would go to her home, or I would have to call her. I finally chose the latter.

Trying to stifle my fury and grief, with my heart breaking into more pieces by the minute, I made the hardest phone call I'd ever made and called Michael's mom.

"Mama Jane," I said, trying to sound calm, "I have some bad news. The police found Michael, but it was too late."

She screamed, "Oh, God, no! Tell me it isn't true!"

Not hiding my tears, I answered, "I'm so sorry." We wept together until I could find my voice. I asked, "Do you want me to send someone down to pick you up and drive you here?"

In between sobs, she answered, "No, I just want to be by myself right now."

I tried to get some rest. It was about 4:00 a.m. by then. Just as my eyes began to droop, I heard Michael's mom come into the house. How she had made the one-and-half hour drive all the way up by herself was beyond me. I met her in the living room, and we just held each other and unleashed the tears.

Still in shock from it all, I realized there was still one very important person I had to tell—Jorjanne. How do you share something like this with a four-year-old? I didn't know what to say.

When she woke up for school, I went into her room, hugged her closely, and told her the grim news. She hugged me like no one else could, and for a long time, we just stayed there in each other's arms. Every depth of my being ached in those moments, but I held back the tears in an attempt to comfort and protect Jorjanne.

The next day, as I prepared to go to the funeral home, I sat on the edge of my bed, thinking about my hellish day.

Trying to sort through the chaos in my mind, I decided to journal. When I opened to the last entry, I was astonished to find these words penned in Michael's handwriting from the day before:

Michael, January 26, 2006

Natalie,

I'm sorry I've brought so much grief and heartache into your life. My heart breaks, but I know the tears will stop. And you and Jorjanne's life will go on. You'll find someone who can take care of you and who is more mentally stable than I am. I'm so confused and so lost. May the Lord who brought this disease welcome me into his kingdom where I'll receive a new body and, hopefully, a new mind. I'm sorry I'm not strong enough, but one day, you'll be thankful I freed you from this living nightmare. Tell Jorjanne I love her, and I pray that she won't have this illness.

I Love You!

Michael

I was shocked! I couldn't believe he had written to me in my journal. He hadn't freed me from a nightmare—he sent me further into the depths. How would I ever live without him? I only wished it was a nightmare—then I could wake up. I couldn't believe the horror of it all. So much had happened in the past twenty-four hours. Michael died and twelve hours later I was planning his funeral. After a sleepless night and hours of guests offering their condolences at our home, I regained my composure and joined my family to go to the funeral home for visitation.

I'm not sure how I made it through the visitation. God carried me when I couldn't walk myself. I sensed supernatural strength and the peace that surpasses understanding. Because of Christ's presence at the funeral home, I found the courage to face the next day at the funeral. I couldn't do it in my own strength, but with Christ's help, I'd make it through the funeral.

As I stood nervously just outside the door to the church, all I could think about was the step I was about to take. This was eerily familiar. As I looked around me at my family, my mom, with tears streaming down her cheeks, whispered into my ear, "I love you." I shifted my weight nervously as the doors opened. There, before me at the altar, was my beloved.

This time, I wasn't walking down the aisle as his bride—but as his widow.

CHAPTER TEN

Telling Jorjanne was the most difficult. I dreaded it. Explaining his illness to a four-year-old had been hard enough. I wanted to protect her from Michael's mood swings as much as possible, but sometimes it was impossible.

When he was manic, she would ask, "Why is Daddy so grumpy?"

"He's sick," I'd explain. "Sometimes when we're sick, we act grumpy. Remember when you had a cold, didn't you feel grumpy?" When he was depressed and stayed in bed, I'd tell her he didn't feel well.

Now Michael's gone, I didn't know what to tell Jorjanne. How could I share such a tragedy with her? Should I tell her, "Daddy killed himself?" Would it be best to say it was an accident? No, I was determined not to lie to her.

I found myself angry with Michael for leaving me behind to pick up the pieces from his death. Not only did I have to deal with the funeral, finances, and a boatload of other stuff, but it was up to me to tell our precious little girl about this horrific event. It just wasn't fair.

Michael died in the wee hours of the morning. When she went to bed the night before, Jorjanne knew her daddy had been hiking and the police were trying to find him. I waited for Jorjanne to wake up before telling her about her daddy's death. My home was already beginning to fill with visitors, so we talked in her room.

I got down on my knees and looked her in the eyes and said, "Sweetheart, the police finally found your daddy last night, and when they did, it was too late. Daddy died last night, sweetie." I paused for a minute to let the truth sink in before continuing.

A few months before Michael's death, we lost our family dog, Gabby. "I am so sorry, baby. Do you remember when our dog Gabby died? Remember how we were sad, and we all cried. We are all sad about Daddy too. It's OK to cry. You may see a lot of people crying, and that's OK. It only means they are sad because they will miss Daddy. If you need to cry, it's OK."

I couldn't believe I was having this conversation. Last night had been hard enough, trying to shield her from the phone calls and the police visits. I wondered how we would ever survive.

"Jorjanne, Daddy lives in heaven now. One day we will see him again, but until then, it will be just the two of us. We'll both look forward to seeing him one day in heaven."

At first, she thought this meant Daddy was on a trip and would come home. As time passed, and she realized he wasn't coming home, she would ask me if we could go visit him. Those were tough questions. How do you explain to a four-year-old she won't see her daddy again on this earth? We read children's books about death, and gradually, reality began to sink in for her—Daddy wasn't coming back.

The first two years were difficult for Jorjanne. She would cry a lot at bedtime, asking for Michael. I'd comfort her as best I could. Then we would pray and ask God to give Daddy messages from us. At Christmas, his birthday, and Father's Day, we bought balloons and let them float up toward heaven for Daddy, so he would know we were thinking of him. Sometimes, she would draw pictures to send with the balloons. These small things seemed to help her stay connected with her daddy.

Children thrive on routine. I had been a stay-at-home mom, and now I had to return to work to support our family. In August of 2006, Jorjanne started kindergarten, and I started working again. Our routine changed, and Jorjanne did not adapt quickly to it. Her teachers told me she didn't smile at school, and she was extremely quiet. At home, she seemed content and happy, but it was a different story when I wasn't around.

One night, when I put her to bed, the tears began to fall.

"Mama, please don't go. Stay with me. Sleep in my room," she pleaded.

With my heart breaking, I said, "Sweetie, it's OK. I'll just be in the other room. If you get scared later, you can come get me."

She was not satisfied. "Mama, please don't go. I don't want you to leave me like Daddy did."

I felt like I'd been punched in the gut; it took me a few minutes to recover. "Jorjanne, you know I love you with all my heart. I don't have any plans to ever leave you, but you need to know if anything ever happens to me, there is one person who will never, ever leave. God is always, always with us. He is with you at school, and he is with you at home. He never leaves us. I don't plan to go anywhere, but if I do, you have grandparents who love you and would take care of you. You will not be alone. I'm here, sweetheart."

The counselor at school was a great help to us. I could call her with my concerns, and she made meeting with Jorjanne a priority. She played games with Jorjanne, getting her to share her feelings. I was afraid my daughter might stifle her emotions to protect me. She didn't like to see me cry. Talking with her counselor at school gave her a safe place to be real without fear of upsetting me.

Once Jorjanne and I settled into a new routine, she gradually adjusted to our new life. Her happy-go-lucky personality returned, and soon she was smiling and laughing again. She loved the television show, *American*

Idol. She would dress up and perform for anyone who would watch and then ask us, "Am I going to Hollywood?" Sometimes she sang her very best but other times, she would intentionally squeal or sing off key. When we told her she didn't make it to Hollywood, she would hang her head and walk away. Five minutes would barely pass before she had changed clothes and was singing again. Her performances gave us both an escape from reality and brought joy into our home. I learned as long as she knew what to expect each day, Jorjanne was content, and her fears something would happen to me began to diminish.

Five years passed, and it became evident to me I needed to tell Jorjanne about how her daddy died. I prayed and asked God to protect her from the details of Michael's death until she was old enough to understand the sickness. God answered my prayer—she never asked how her daddy died. Now she was older. I needed to tell her before she heard the truth from someone else.

As I prepared to tell Jorjanne how her daddy died, I began researching and asking others whose lives had been touched by suicide for advice. It saddened me to realize how many people had been encouraged to protect their children from the truth by lying. Many well-meaning people did this, but it caused the child to experience mistrust. Others were advised to say nothing. One friend told me he was in his twenties before he learned his mother had died by suicide. For years, no one would talk with him about his mother's death. Because no one told the truth, he grew up thinking his father murdered his mother. He grew up not trusting his father. All of this could have been avoided with the truth.

I was convinced more than ever Jorjanne needed to hear about Michael's death from me. I asked several friends to pray with me that God would give me the words and the timing to do this. Finally, the time seemed right.

Jorjanne was eight, almost nine, and was painting a birdhouse at the kitchen table. I was cleaning in my bedroom, and the Holy Spirit prompted me to tell her about Michael. I joined her at the table and began talking about the book I was writing.

"Do you know what Mama's book is about?" I asked her.

"Yes," she said. "It's about your life."

I continued, "That's right. It's about my life with your daddy. God has been so good to us since Daddy died. We've had some hard times, and some days have been really rough, but God has helped us in so many ways. Mama is writing this book so others who are hurting will know God can help them too. I want them to experience the joy we have experienced."

I braced myself for what I knew I needed to say next. I decided to just say it. "Jorjanne, do you know how your daddy died?"

She looked up at me with those big brown eyes and responded, "He was really sick."

Taking a deep breath, I said, "That's true, honey. Your daddy was very sick. He had an illness called bipolar disorder, which affected his brain. Do you remember when you were little, you had an imaginary friend named Sukey?"

She nodded.

"You knew deep down Sukey wasn't real, but you would pretend that he was there." Again, she nodded.

"Well, your Daddy's brain was very confused. He would hear imaginary voices talking to him, and he would think they were real. One day, Daddy was really sad and confused. He heard voices talking to him, and he was so confused he killed himself."

She inhaled deeply and just stared ahead.

"Honey, this is called suicide."

Her shoulders shuddered as she continued to listen.

"I want you to know your Daddy loved you so very much. He absolutely adored you, and he never, ever stopped loving you. You had nothing to do with Daddy's death. He was very sick. If he had been healthy, he would never have taken his life. Never ever forget how much Daddy loved you."

We talked some more, and I said, "If you ever have any questions about your daddy and what happened, ask me. I will tell you anything you want to know. I promise to tell you the truth."

She nodded. The discussion ended.

This experience reinforced for me honesty is worthwhile. I never wanted Jorjanne to feel I'd lied to her—so I didn't. I've told her the truth in increments she could handle. As she grew older, the questions changed. One day in middle school she came home sobbing and slammed the door exclaiming, "I'm never going back to school. Never!" Shocked by her outburst, I asked her what happened. She told me her friend Cassidy said, "Jorjanne, somebody told me your daddy killed himself. I told them he did not and not to lie about something like that. I stood up for you."

"What did you say?" I asked.

"I didn't know what to say, so I didn't say anything," Jorjanne replied.

"Jorjanne, you don't have to say anything you don't want to say. When people ask about your dad, tell them you don't like talking about him and then stop. You don't owe anyone an explanation."

This soon became her normal response.

Jorjanne is in college now, and she has shared the story of losing her dad with others to help them in their own grief. She is still healing, but she has come a long way.

The biggest thing for me in telling Jorjanne when she was younger was to help her understand her daddy was sick. He was not thinking clearly, or he would have never taken his life.

I also wanted to point Jorjanne to God's goodness. Even though Michael's death was a tragedy in our lives, God has given us joy since then.

CHAPTER ELEVEN

Seven years after Michael's death, my prayers began to change. I remembered the Scriptures talking about the seventh year as the Year of Jubilee. I began to ask God to make 2013 a year of jubilee in my life. To my shock (although I shouldn't have been surprised by God's answers to my prayers), God brought a friend back into my life who related to my heartache.

I had not seen Jeff in years. He had also served with the North American Mission Board and was good friends with Michael. When I received a message on Facebook asking if he could call me, I thought Michael's friend wanted to check on his widow. Boy, was I surprised to find out I was wrong.

Months after sending me the Facebook message, Jeff finally called. After checking in to see how I was doing, Jeff told me he was living in Virginia.

"No way," I said. "I'm going to graduate school in Virginia."

We continued to talk, and he asked me if he could call me again. When I said, "Sure," he responded.

"I want to make myself clear. I want to call you as a guy interested in you. Can I call you again?"

I was stunned. Jeff was interested in me. We continued to talk on the phone for the next few weeks and made plans to drive over to Lynchburg so we could meet up when I went to Virginia for my weeklong intensive class.

For our first date, Jeff and I went to an ice-skating rink. We planned to skate, but we missed the window for open skate, so we sat in the bleachers and talked. He told me about his family, and we realized we had a great deal in common. Jeff described his mom's struggles with bipolar disorder; he understood the chaos the disorder could create.

We continued our conversation over dinner, then talked more over coffee. I didn't want the night to end.

Jeff took me back to my friends' home where I was staying, and he hugged me goodnight. I had barely gotten into the house when the phone rang. It was Jeff. "Natalie, I don't want to wait to see you again. Can I come back next weekend and see you?" My plan was to drive back to Georgia on Friday afternoon, but I didn't hesitate in answering him. "Sure, I can stick around until Sunday."

Jeff came back the following weekend. We hiked. He played guitar. We sang together. We went to a Jars of Clay concert. While all these activities were fun, none compared to the excitement I felt in this budding friendship with Jeff. When I got home, a friend came up to me grinning. "I see how it's going to be. You're keeping secrets from me." I asked her what she meant. "I had to read about it on Facebook. You are in a relationship."

What? A relationship. What was she talking about? She opened her Facebook account and showed me Jeff had changed his status from single to in a relationship. Well, I guess I didn't have to wonder how he felt. I knew I liked him—a lot—but we never talked about dating exclusively. I called Jeff that afternoon and told him I couldn't make our dating relationship official until he came to visit and spent some time with Jorjanne. He came to visit me in Georgia the following month. I loved watching him with Jorjanne. We went to a corn maze, and he joined in the silliness as we played follow the leader in the maze. We laughed, and when we traded stories, I felt a kinship like I had with no other.

One story Jeff shared with me demonstrates the turmoil mania created in his family. One time he thrust himself across the back seat, desperate to stop his mom, Sherrie, from pulling on the door handle as she tried to get out of the moving car. His mom wrestled to push Jeff back as she tried to exit the moving vehicle. Jeff wondered how they had gotten to this point. Sherrie was frantic. She was desperate. No seventeen-year-old should see his mom in such a terrible state. She wanted to escape from the car. She knew they were taking her to a psychiatric institution, and she was frenzied. Sherrie wanted freedom from mental illness.

Running his fingers through his hair, he prayed begging God to help his mom.

When they arrived at the hospital, Dennis, Jeff's stepfather, went inside while Jeff waited in the car with his mom. She began to swing into a more lucid state as it began to register that her behavior was scaring Jeff. "I am so sorry, Jeff. I love you. I am going to get better. You'll see. I will get better." In these moments, Jeff had glimpses of his real mom versus her psychosis. This was comforting to him even in the chaos.

Jeff tried to reassure his mom everything would be okay as she was admitted to the hospital. He was able to keep his emotions in check until he left the hospital. Needing a break from the chaos, Jeff drove to his dad's house, one-and-a-half hours away. Then the tears were unleashed. Jeff's tears were coupled with sadness and anguish as he feared for his mom's life and his mom's sanity.

Jeff soon learned his mom suffered from bipolar disorder. What seemed like a crazy cycle with his mom was actually a manic episode.

Now a diagnosis had been given, things began to make more sense. Jeff could recall periods when his mom would cry and wanted to stay in bed all day. She had been struggling with depressive episodes, but Jeff and his brother had always gone to stay with their dad or grandmother, so they had been sheltered from her pervasive mood swings.

Jeff and I had both experienced heartache and pain and longed for a new beginning. God had been working behind the scenes in both of our lives to bring us to such a time as this.

Seven months later we were married.

CHAPTER TWELVE

In the following years, bipolar disorder ravaged Jeff's relationship with his mother. He was always questioning whether she was taking her medications. Sherrie's disability continued to impact her quality of life.

I'd love to say because I'm a licensed professional counselor, I knew exactly what to do to improve Sherrie's quality of life, but it wouldn't be true. Sherrie knew about Michael's suicide, and often apologized to me for what Michael had done. She could relate to his pain. She, too, had attempted to take her own life multiple times and had survived. When she was well, she would share how she could never do such a thing. Unfortunately, the periods of wellness were often short-lived.

Sherrie coped with the constant mood swings by self-medicating. She would play around with different medications to feel better. In time, she began to struggle with chronic pain. She'd go to multiple doctors for pain management and gained access to a variety of narcotics. She abused the medications, which only compounded her problems.

She was stopped by police multiple times for reckless driving while under the influence of prescription pain medicine and was continually let go with a warning. We suspect they showed her mercy because of her age, and she lived in a senior adult community. Sherrie was secretive about the offenses but would often tell of the incidents months later.

Sherrie struggled financially. When she was manic, she would spend large amounts of money for no reason. Her spending habits brought back memories of Michael's excessive spending. Exorbitant spending is a common characteristic of mania. Jeff and I both felt the frustrations from watching our loved ones spend impulsively. There was a time when Michael and I had three cars and he came home from an auction and told me he had bought a fourth one. I was livid. We barely had money to pay our bills, and he bought a car we didn't need. Imagine my fury when I learned this new-to-us car didn't run. His spending habits wreaked havoc in our lives.

Sherrie often borrowed money from loan sharks and had to depend on family to bail her out when she couldn't pay them back. Jeff and his brother were concerned about her driving after all the incidents with police, but before they could intervene, her car was repossessed by the bank. From that day forward, Sherrie would no longer drive. We felt relieved, for we lived in constant fear she'd have a fatal accident.

After Jeff and I were married, we lived three-and-a-half hours from Sherrie. His brother, who lived in the same town, took over most of her caregiving. There were times when Sherrie would call Jeff's brother, Scott, three or four times a day. Jeff and I felt both guilt and relief at not being able to help more. At times when Jeff would call her, she was confused; at other times she was clear-headed. Sherrie began saying she was hurting badly, and sometimes she felt like she just wanted to die. She would repeatedly ask, "Why is this happening to me?"

Our concerns mounted when one of Sherrie's neighbors called Jeff's brother to express her concern. She had gone into Sherrie's apartment earlier and found Sherrie sitting in a chair naked. When the neighbor asked what she was doing, Sherrie answered flatly, "I don't know." Her neighbor encouraged her to get dressed, so she did. Then she fell asleep in the same chair. We believed Sherrie would sleep it off and be better in the morning. Sherrie had probably taken a few too many pain pills or muscle relaxers, which was common at the time.

The next day, Scott called Jeff to inform him Sherrie had been found unconscious in her room and was on a ventilator in ICU. We raced to pack our things and drove to the hospital. Scott told us Sherrie had overdosed, taking two weeks' worth of medicines in a forty-eight to sixty-hour period. She had been in the hospital for suicide attempts so many times, we felt sure she would be okay. Sherrie was suffering from serotonin syndrome and was unresponsive for days. We spent the days at the hospital with her. The doctors asked us if Sherrie had a living will. She did not. We prayed God would either heal her or take her home.

Eventually she regained consciousness. When she was alert, she would hallucinate, and her words were incoherent. When talking, Sherrie seemed to pick a few topics and repeat the same thing in loops. One minute, she would talk about how she had killed herself and was dead. Next, she would deny having attempted suicide. The emotional toll on our family was exhausting. We were unsure whether she would survive and wondered what sort of life she would have if she did.

Sherrie did survive and went to rehab as she recovered. She was eventually able to live on her own again. Because of the excessive prescription pain medication abuse and subsequent suicide attempt, Jeff and Scott moved Sherrie into a senior living facility with medication management. The months of med management were fruitful and hopeful for Sherrie and her family. She lost some independence when she stopped driving, and she lost additional independence when she moved to a new facility. But she gained a considerable respite from her prescription drug abuse. Jeff's mom channeled a lot of anger and frustration when she lost portions of her independence initially. She later grew to appreciate her living situation.

After a period of relative calm, we began to believe Sherrie was at last taking her medications as prescribed and was living well. Our visits were pleasant and uneventful. This in and of itself was a gift. Soon things began to turn south. Sherrie once again started seeking pain medications from various medical professionals. Our concern grew. Jeff and Scott made plans to meet with her the following day. It was too late.

Two hundred acetaminophen tablets—that is the amount of medication we believe Jeff's mother ingested prior to her death. After forty years of living with mental illness, battling an endless list of health problems (some physical, some emotional), and fighting for her life, Sherrie lost her life to her unquiet mind. Jeff's mom lost her life to bipolar disorder. She had made attempts in the past and was hospitalized for multiple weeks. She always managed to pull through. Sadly, on March 10, 2018, she died.

Here are excerpts from the eulogy Jeff shared at her funeral. They give great insight into the woman she was apart from her disorder:

> I want to say a few kind words about Sherrie. A mother. A grandmother. A daughter. A sister. Sometimes the life of the party. At her core, she was an amazing, creative, and talented woman. Her humor was razor sharp at times. We were blessed to celebrate sixty years of life with mom.

> Mom had a great laugh, a sometimes-questionable sense of humor, a sincere love for her family; in her younger years, an unmatched homemaker, a fun-loving spirit; in her working years, an unshakable work ethic.

> At the end of Mom's life, on the final day of her life,

> She was worried ...

> She was uncomfortable ...

She was troubled …

She told me she wasn't sure where she was … .

Because of the cross and the empty tomb, we know

Mom was worried … she doesn't have to worry anymore.

Mom was uncomfortable … she has no discomfort anymore.

Mom was troubled … she has no trouble anymore.

Mom was confused and unsure of her whereabouts … she knows she is at rest now in the presence of God, who loves her, and she is in the presence of God whom she loved.

She was a worrier. But now there is nothing to worry about. She endured illness, hurts, and anguish. For her all of this is past. Most of Mom's hardships were health related. Now Mom is at peace. No more physical hurts. No more mental pains. No more unquiet mind. Mom is at peace.

Together we have faced tremendous pain, but I am so grateful we were able to face Sherrie's death together. We continue to seek out support from others who have experienced suicide loss, especially at Survivors of Suicide (SOS) meetings.[1] We aren't walking the path of suicide bereavement alone. I praise God for my marriage to Jeff and for his relationship with Jorjanne. Despite our hurts and pains, we are experiencing the precious grace of God in our family. God is indeed a good God. He is still on the throne, and yes, we can trust him.

CHAPTER THIRTEEN

When a person experiences great loss, grief is a very healthy and normal reaction. I had never experienced such devastating grief before losing Michael, so I really didn't understand what it meant to grieve. I thought grief meant sadness. My counselor explained to me there are six stages of grief. I came to see I had begun the grieving process while Michael was still alive. His illness had stolen him from me, and I knew, even while he was living, I'd already lost the man I loved.

The first stage is denial or shock. In the first weeks after Michael's death, I'd find myself picking up the phone and dialing his number, momentarily forgetting he was gone. Throughout the day, I would think of things I needed to tell him. I knew rationally he was gone, but on a subconscious level, I often forgot. It took time for the finality of his death to penetrate, moving me into another stage in the grief process.

The second stage is anger. It's crazy how we can believe in God's sovereignty and his goodness with our minds, yet our emotions can roar with anger toward him at the same time. "Why God? Why me?" I must have asked myself a hundred times. After all, I'd given my life to serving him. What did I have to show for it? My husband was dead, and I was left behind as a single parent with no job. Was I angry? You bet I was! The crazy thing is I was afraid to admit my anger was at God. I was a missionary, and I loved God. I thought being mad at God wrong. I finally realized, right or wrong, I was mad, and I was only denying it. I was finally honest with myself and with God about my anger. I found refuge in the book of Psalms, especially as I read about David's repeated anger toward God and others.

Not only was I mad at God, but I was also mad at Michael and at myself. I blamed myself for not being able to do something to prevent this. I accused Michael of being selfish and uncaring.

Most of my anger toward Michael came while he was still alive. It infuriated me he would stop taking his medicines. He knew he was sick, and yet he wanted to be well so badly he refused to admit his illness was chronic. His erratic behavior kept us on a roller coaster much of the time. There were times I hated him.

One month after Michael's death, I wrote this to Michael in my journal:

> I feel as if half of me has been ripped out. I miss you so much. Today, Jorjanne didn't go to school, and I am exhausted. I need your help. She needs you. Why did you leave us? I know you thought you were helping us by freeing us from your illness, but you were wrong. We need you! No matter how much I pray, beg, and plead, you are not coming back, and I hate it. My life seems empty without you. I look around the house and you are there. I go outside and you are there. Everything reminds me of you—only you aren't here.
>
> I'm used to being able to make things better, but I can't. Nothing I do will bring you back. We were supposed to get old together. You stole this from us—if not you, then this stupid illness! I hate it! I feel so much right now that I can't decipher what I am feeling. I'm angry that I have to deal with all the junk and that I have to face life without my best friend. I'm mad that you are in heaven, freed from pain, while I am left here, overwhelmed with hurt.

So much of my life was about you that I don't know who I am anymore. Psalm 56:8 tells me that God bottles our tears; he must have a room full of my bottles because the tears won't stop coming. Oh Michael, you were such a great man! That is what makes losing you so hard!!

I wish I could say I dealt with my anger all at once, and it didn't return, but that wouldn't be true. The stages are more like a staircase. We move up and down the stages throughout the grief process. It is not a linear progression. Years later, I still find myself angry at Michael about what happened.

The third stage is bargaining. When we realize we are losing someone, we try to bargain with God in hopes of more time with the person. I pleaded with God to heal Michael. I couldn't understand why God would allow this illness and, ultimately, Michael's suicide to happen. We were serving God. We were trying to live our lives in obedience to him. I felt like God wasn't keeping his end of the bargain. I grew up believing if I lived a moral life—did the right things and went to church—good things would happen. My faulty theology was no longer working for me. I felt I was obeying God, and yet my family was crumbling around me.

What I didn't realize at the time is God doesn't owe us anything. He is God. He is good. He is trustworthy. He is sovereign. Years later, my pastor said, "If God never gave us any other blessings, he has already given us more than we deserve." I had to really ponder his words. He was right. In giving me salvation, God had already blessed me with far more than I could ever deserve. Who was I to question his goodness?

I had read the book of Job multiple times, but never had I really internalized the fact bad things happen to all people, no matter how we live. Praise God, he didn't give me what I deserved (judgment and wrath) but instead gave me a great gift—his presence in the midst of the trials. These truths later gave me peace, but there were times when I felt like God had betrayed me.

Feeling sad is a normal part of the grieving process. Nights were the most difficult for me. I would tuck Jorjanne into bed and go into a quiet room. The silence was maddening. I cried myself to sleep many nights. When the sadness hit during the day, I'd often retreat to the shower where I could cry in solitude. When Jorjanne would ask why my eyes were red, I'd tell her it must be soap in my eyes.

Jorjanne struggled with sadness too. She would continuously ask when her daddy would be home, and when I'd remind her that he was in heaven, she'd cry. "I want to go to heaven and see Daddy." My heart broke each time she said these words.

There are times when grief can trigger depression. When the sadness is severe enough to disrupt a person's life, it becomes depression. Thankfully, my grief did not turn into depression.

When I think of grief, I think of Naomi from the Old Testament book of Ruth. Her life is an excellent example of someone who experienced hardship as well as grief, which led to depression. Death took her husband and her two sons, leaving Naomi with no other choice than to return to her homeland. She even told her daughters-in-law, "the hand of the Lord has gone forth against me." Naomi discouraged the girls from traveling with her. After all, God seemed to have it out for her. Despite Naomi's words, Ruth solemnly swore to follow her anyway. Once they reached Bethlehem, Naomi changed her name to Mara, which means "bitter." She believed the Almighty had dealt bitterly with her. If God was in control of everything, wasn't he to blame for all the bitter things she had experienced? If God loved her, why would he have let these things happen?

When Michael died, I was overcome with grief. Life as I knew it had ended. How in the world would I go on? I did move on, one day at a time.

The same was true for Naomi. While Naomi experienced great hardship and sadness, she did not despair. She made a plan to return to Bethlehem. She kept going; she did not give up. She was uncertain what was ahead, but she knew God was with the people in Bethlehem. She knew her hope came from the Lord, but she also blamed him for her current troubles. She blamed God for emptying her life and making her bitter.

Once we accept our loved one's death as reality, we're able to move forward. I will never forget my "moment of acceptance." As the one-year anniversary of Michael's death approached, my friends asked me what I wanted to do. I'd been praying asking God to turn my mourning into laughing and my crying into dancing. Without overthinking, I exclaimed, "I want to go dancing." I had recently discovered contradancing, which is similar to square dancing but instead of moving around a square, you dance up and down a line.

On the anniversary of his death, I went to Atlanta with friends to dance. We were laughing and having a grand time when the caller made an announcement. "We are thrilled to have a group from North Georgia dancing with us tonight. What are you guys celebrating?" In that moment, I wanted to crawl under a rock. Celebrating? It was the anniversary of my husband's suicide, and he thought I was celebrating. What kind of sick wife am I? As I bent at the waist and stared at the floor, the Holy Spirit spoke to my heart. "Natalie, what did you pray for?" In that instant, I realized that God had answered my prayer. Michael had been gone for a year, but my life continued. I knew at that moment—I had accepted the loss.

We never "get over" losing someone we care about, but hopefully, we get to a place where God can use our loss to transform us and to help others. I learned to take things one step at a time.

My counselor taught me the importance of feeling, saying, "Feelings aren't good or bad—they just are."

She told me, "When you want to cry, cry. When you find yourself laughing, enjoy it; don't feel guilty. Let others help you. Don't try to make it on your own." Her words granted me freedom.

Physical well-being is also important. A friend gave me a one-year membership to the gym when Michael died, and this was the best gift she could have given me. Not only was it great for me physically but also mentally. Exercise is a great form of stress release.

Suicide bereavement differs from other types of grief because we often struggle with explosive emotions: guilt, fear, and shame—well beyond the limits experienced in other types of deaths. The grief of losing Michael and Sherrie was much more complicated than other losses I have experienced. It shut down my normal coping mechanisms, causing added (often scary) feelings of, "What's wrong with me?" I didn't know it at the time, but survivors of suicide loss rank among the highest risk of suicide as we are nine times more likely to die by suicide than the general population. Unfortunately, Michael's suicide led to a string of other suicide deaths in his family, not because of genetics but because of exposure.

The guilt after losing Michael was suffocating at times. I knew Michael was depressed, but I had no idea how tormented he was until I read his journals after his death. I often wondered what I might have done differently if I had known. I can honestly say the "what ifs" can consume us. There comes a time when we need to let go of the guilt. We cannot judge decisions we made in the past based on knowledge we have now. We need to forgive ourselves for things we may have done wrong and cannot change.

Recording my thoughts in a journal was great for helping me sort out how I really thought and felt about what happened. It helped me to process the guilt, the embarrassment, the rejection, and the shame. It also helped me to let go of my anger and resentment over Michael's decision to abandon us. Journaling was therapeutic for me.

CHAPTER FOURTEEN

Why is it that when a family member dies of cancer, friends rush to offer their support, but when a loved one dies from a self-inflicted act, people hesitate to respond? During the pain of losing both Michael and Sherrie, it was critical for me to know others cared and weren't judging. Where were our friends?

The feeling of rejection by friends and family was real. People didn't know what to say, so they completely avoided me, deepening my feelings of aloneness and rejection. Was I being shunned because of Michael's act? I felt shame and guilt when I would go out in public. Did others believe I caused his death? In fact, some of my friends avoided calling me, then later told me they were afraid they might "fall apart" and upset me. I had no way of knowing their feelings. I felt they either didn't care or were ashamed to talk to me.

During those early days, I needed people to be with me and sometimes to cry with me. I didn't want people who had it all together. I longed for people who could relate to my pain to come alongside me and offer support. I ached physically as I wondered if I was the only person to ever experience such devastating loss. I knew rationally my belief was unfounded but knowing the truth did not take away my agony. Paul writes in Romans 12:15, we are to mourn with those who mourn. Even Jesus wept when

Lazarus died (John 11:35). Some of the greatest comfort I received during the dark time was when my friends stayed near and cried with me.

I've learned everyone grieves in their own way. Some want others to rally around them and offer support, while others just want to be left alone. At times, I wanted people to reach out, and yet, there were other instances when I just wanted to be left alone. I appreciated those who honored my wishes for time alone but didn't forget about me. Friends continued to reach out to me via texts, cards, and emails and gave me time and space to grieve, but also reminded me they were available when I needed them.

Far too many survivors have said to me they had ample emotional support in the first year, but then the help fell away—people no longer called or talked about the person who died. The inconsistency left many of my friends with suicide loss feeling isolated and alone. While time alone is important, I learned long-term isolation is dangerous when you are grieving. There were times I had to fight the urge to isolate. Even if I didn't feel like talking to anyone, I would go to a park or a store and walk around; these were ways for me to be around people without talking to them.

Emotional support was a godsend, but so was the practical help that I received from caring friends and family. When I felt least capable of processing what to do next or handling a task that felt overwhelming, someone would show up and help.

I waited until the morning after Michael's death to tell my daughter, Jorjanne, her daddy was dead. We were both grief-stricken. Less than an hour later, friends appeared, offering to keep her for the day. It was a monumental relief knowing she would be protected from things she was too young to understand.

On the day of the memorial visitation, another family took her to see the musical *Annie*. I still can't express the emotions I felt when she came home that night, singing about the sun coming out tomorrow. Even in my despair, I saw a glimmer of God among us.

Another set of friends kept Jorjanne during the funeral. Even though they were grieving with me, they were willing to set aside their own pain and care for my daughter during our time of need. This practical act of kindness expressed love to me in a very tangible way.

I remember sitting in my living room just hours before the funeral, talking with people who cared. One of them asked me what my favorite comfort food was. I had never really thought about that, but I told her sometimes I crave Zero candy bars. A little while later, she left with another friend, and when they returned, they brought me a bag full of Zero bars. They had gone to every gas station nearby and bought all they found. This meant so much to me and continued to comfort me in the following weeks.

There were other times when I felt God's presence in the kindness of people around me. For instance, a dear friend stayed with me the entire first week after Michael died and answered phone calls. It was too painful for me to repeatedly explain what had happened, so she did it. She also addressed and mailed notes of thanks for me. That was huge. My heart was broken, and my brain was fried. I was emotionally incapable of writing stacks of letters to those who deserved my gratitude, so she intervened for me.

Because I was a stay-at-home mom, there were financial concerns. I was frightened because there would no longer be an income, and I wasn't sure how I could quickly replace it. Bills needed to be paid, and I had no job. While I was at the funeral home, I learned his life insurance might be invalidated because the cause of death was self-inflicted. How would I pay for the funeral? I was consumed with worry.

In a surprising and incredibly generous gesture, Michael's employer picked up the expense of his funeral. Sitting at the funeral home, with my head in my hands, I prayed in anguish asking God how I would pay.

"Natalie, Doug just called," my friend, Bonnie, said. I lifted my head. "The funeral expenses have just been paid."

"How?"

"He said Michael's employer covered the cost." I cried again—this time in relief.

It humbled me to know they cared about Michael and me so much. It was an act of God's grace, and I felt comforted to experience such loving care. My family and friends felt like the hands and feet of Jesus to me during those first few months. I would have been lost without them.

Our church recognized the need for swift assistance and set up a bank account to help. To process the necessary paperwork, I had to go to the bank within days of my husband's death. I fought to keep my composure, as I suppressed the urge to fall into the floor and sob, while I made financial decisions that would impact the future. I was glad my mom went with me. Having her beside me gave me courage to face the day. She was also able to clearly explain what seemed muddled to me during so much confusion and grief.

There seemed to be no escape from the details demanding my attention and inspiring fresh occasions to mourn.

When Michael's death certificate arrived, it was not subtle about the cause of death, and it devastated me to see the specifics in writing: "Death by gunshot wound to head." The coroner gave me his personal effects. I saw the newly missing arm of his eyeglasses, I felt I would collapse all over again. *Can I bear more grief?* The grief felt like more than I could endure. I wanted my world to restore itself to normalcy. For my daughter to have a daddy. For me to grow old with my husband, like all the fairytales promise.

Yet curling up and refusing to face our new reality wasn't an option. Even as I struggled to deal with loss, I also had to confront my own shame and fury. Each time I had to present someone with a copy of the death certificate, I felt embarrassed. It never occurred to me, at the time, to take someone with me to handle the logistics of Michael's death. I wasn't thinking clearly about much of anything. Little did I know what fierce pain those small things would cause.

Surely, I reasoned, I could go to the phone company by myself. Did the cell phone company really need to know I was canceling his account because he completed suicide? Why was it necessary to show evidence of his death to the electric company, and why did I have to pay a new deposit to change the power bill over to my name? It wasn't their business how my husband died. When the clerk read the death certificate, she looked up at me with pity, which left me feeling shamed all over again. She didn't say a word. She didn't have to. Her face said it all—she felt sorry for me. I hung my head low and rushed out the door.

When the time came to clean out Michael's closet and his belongings, a group of ladies from my Bible study came over to assist me. Facing this difficult task was easier being surrounded by friends who cared. I remember sitting in the middle of Michael's closet and sobbing. They didn't pressure me to stop or to get back to work. They were present with me in my pain. Those ladies let me talk when I wanted to talk. They cried with me when I needed release. They left me alone when I needed to be quiet and reflect. They were heaven-sent.

After the initial shock wore off, letters and cards were balm for my gaping wounds. It was comforting to know that others missed Michael, too, and didn't condemn him. I wanted people to remember my husband for the amazing man he was—not as that guy who committed suicide.

At his funeral, I asked people to write their favorite "Michael" stories so that someday, I could share them with our daughter. I gathered all the stories together into two three-ring binders. I bought clear sleeves to protect the stories. Their tributes were such a blessing to me. When I became overcome with grief and loneliness, I read through their recollections, and even now, I often laugh as they shed light on the precious man I married. Jorjanne knows about the notebooks filled with stories, but she is not yet ready to read them. I will keep this treasure for her until she decides she wants them.

One friend wasn't quite sure how to help me heal but was determined to send encouragement. Every morning, without fail, she emailed a different Scripture verse to me. Kim gave no commentary—she simply quoted the verse. Her plan worked. It meant a lot to know she was praying for me each day, and I began to look forward to opening my inbox. What she sent was simple, yet profound, and offered healing to my wounded soul.

CHAPTER FIFTEEN

The first year after his death was the hardest for me. It was an excruciating cycle of firsts: my first Valentine's Day as a widow, my first birthday without Michael, Jorjanne's first birthday without her daddy, Father's Day, Christmas, our anniversary, and his birthday. It seemed that every time I would begin to get a foothold on coping, a fresh reminder would surface on the calendar. They were all difficult days.

Unlike Kim's encouraging emails, there were well-meaning people who tried to "fix things" by quoting Scripture. They would say, "And we know that in all things God works for the good of those who love him" (Romans 8:28). People assured me that based on this Scripture, everything would be okay. At the time, it felt offensive to me because the assumption seemed to be that I should automatically, as a Christian, be accepting and look for the good in Michael's death. While many things would eventually shift to become more bearable, all was certainly not okay. My world had collapsed around me, and I didn't know what to do. No one could give me my husband back. No one could restore my daughter's father.

I ached for others to acknowledge my pain and to support me through it. God heard my prayers, and sent some wise individuals who, by honoring my pain, made those "firsts" more bearable. Those who phoned and sent notes of concern and prayer meant the world to me. I felt comforted knowing others hadn't forgotten Michael or me.

I was particularly worried about the first Valentine's Day without him. A precious group of friends planned a special brunch so I would be surrounded with love. The table was brightly decorated, and the atmosphere was lighthearted. We made homemade greeting cards, which helped focus my attention on something other than my loss. They presented me with a wooden chest decoupaged with one of my favorite paintings as a place to stow special mementos. Then the women each gave me a letter describing their favorite memories of Michael.

Though my heart ached for him, they had transformed a day I had dreaded into a blessing. Instead of focusing on what I had lost, their thoughtful efforts reminded me anew of much that remained special in my life. Left alone, I probably would have wallowed around in self-pity. They made sure that didn't happen.

I would be remiss if I did not mention the most important relationship for promoting resilience and posttraumatic growth in my life—my relationship with God. For believers in Christ, we are never alone. We serve a God who will never leave us or forsake us. He is Immanuel, God with us. Trusting in God's sovereignty gives hope for tomorrow.

Reading the Bible daily is always important, but the practice became my lifeline after Michael's death.

When you lose someone to suicide, you immediately begin to question, "Why?" Having immersed myself in the research and working with numerous survivors, I've come to realize this is the wrong question. Even if we find an answer to why, it doesn't negate our pain. The question we need to ask ourselves in the wake of suicide is "What now?" As we search to find something—anything—good in the situation, healing ensues. Viktor Frankl, a Holocaust survivor, and the founder of Logotherapy, said it well. "In some ways suffering ceases to be suffering at the moment it finds a meaning, such as the meaning of a sacrifice."[1] It was only after I accepted the reality of the Michael's death, that I could begin to move forward.

CHAPTER SIXTEEN

How do we even start to reframe or make sense of the loss? One of the first things I had to do was purge. To make sense of Michael's death, I had to express my thoughts and feelings before I could process and release them.

My personal purging process began two months after Michael's death, when Jorjanne and I went to Mexico on a mission trip. One of our first assignments was to find a place to be alone and to spend one and a half hours with God. Until then, I had filled my life with activity. Every time I got quiet, I fell apart. Jorjanne was with me on the trip, and I was relieved I could get out of the required "quiet time" because I had to care for her. As we were leaving to find a place of solitude, a friend told me Jorjanne had fallen asleep, and she would watch her while I spent some time alone with God.

My life was filled with fury. I finally unleashed all the tears hovering inside me since the funeral. I had fought to maintain my composure for so long I was shocked by all the tears and anguish I felt during the time alone. Once I'd been honest with God and with myself, I felt emptied emotionally. I decided to go for a walk.

I was walking alone in a huge field when I came upon a plant. It appeared to be dead, blackened, and scorched. As I gazed upon it, I meditated on how symbolic this was of Michael's life. As I looked closer, I saw another plant, just like it, growing up beside it. A small branch growing from this dying plant—green and full of life. On its stem were two beautiful, yellow flowers, with more just waiting to bloom. God spoke to my heart. While Michael's earthly ministry was finished, mine had only begun. God wanted to give me new life and new ministry. He wanted me to grow and bear fruit. The only way for me to do so was to rise above the ashes and remain in the light.

Humbled, I fell to my knees in prayer to God. I was reminded of the story of Jonah. God provided a vine to shade Jonah from the harsh rays of the sun, and later, a worm ate the vine. Jonah complained and blamed God for taking away the vine (Jonah 4:8). I didn't want to be like Jonah. I asked God to help me be thankful for my time with Michael. I asked him to help me not to become bitter over losing him.

This moment was a turning point in my life. I knew God had not forsaken me. He still had a plan for my life. I'm amazed because, even now, whenever I see small yellow flowers, I am reminded of the special time with God. The flowers serve as a reminder of God's abundant love for me— God's love letters to me. I pray the beauty will continue to grow out of the ashes.

Since then, my life has taken a new direction. I have grown to know God in a deeper, more intimate way. Before Michael's illness and death, I'd never been in a place of desperation. In the past, I'm sure I gave people "pat" answers to their problems and said I would pray for them (though I confess, many times I did not). Now that I know what it is like to hurt deeply, I'm more compassionate to others who are hurting.

Beginning to write *Seeking Answers* allowed me a place to express and purge my anguish and my heartache over losing Michael. Talking with other survivors and attending Survivors of Suicide (SOS) meetings provided support to discuss and process subsequent suicidal losses. Other survivors discussed how journaling allowed them a private place to emotionally expel all the turmoil in their heads, while others did this publicly through blogging. When asked how journaling helped, one survivor explained, "It definitely was a huge tool in healing to write it down, whether it was electronically writing it down or physically writing it down. Had I not written all of that down, I probably wouldn't remember."

I often ask my counseling clients to write a letter to the person who died. While this exercise can be very painful it has the potential to propel individuals into deeper healing. Writing down thoughts and feelings seemed to be a healthy way of purging the pain. While I didn't write Michael a letter, I began writing our story in hopes of one day giving it to Jorjanne. You are reading some of those thoughts now as you hold this book in your hand. The process was therapeutic for me. Other times, I'd talk to God and ask him to tell Michael about my days. Some people choose to talk to the person they lost, telling them about their days and their emotional pain. The key for me was to get it out. Stuffing our pain does not lead to healing, but instead stifles our ability to progress in our grief.

Unfortunately, there is no short cut through the pain; we must release the hurt, the resentment, the bitterness, and all the other emotions associated with the suicidal loss.

The journey is difficult. Kristen described it well:

> I think the best things I learned is not to hide. If we're going to really do grief well, for lack of a better word, we must be open to the pain. Who said, "The best way to get to the light is to plunge right into the darkness?" I think this is true. We must take the plunge. It hurts and we don't want to experience it—nobody likes pain. To fully grieve well, we need to face the pain head on, whatever that means.[1]

Purging the pain is a necessary part of making sense of the loss and moving forward.

In addition, to purging, church involvement helped me to make sense of my loss. I often tell people the church was the hands and feet of Jesus in my life after Michael's death.

Frequently, I've heard, "A faith not tested is a faith not trusted," and I believe this is true. I can't tell you how many people have told me it is wrong to question God, and I want to say, "Have you read the Psalms?" The Bible is full of examples of godly people questioning God—God is big enough to handle our queries. He knows our heart even if we say our thoughts out loud. He encourages us to be real and honest before him.

I've heard other survivors say one of their greatest challenges is going to church after the loss. "Everyone at church seems to have it all together," said one woman. "I just can't bring myself to put on a happy face and greet others."

Going to church after losing Michael was a challenge. I could not "keep it together." I cried almost every Sunday for a year. I would be feeling strong, then the choir would sing a song about heaven. I would lose it. Many times, I ran out of the sanctuary to the bathroom to sob. Most of the time, someone else would follow me and cry with me.

My church allowed me to be real with my pain. No one expected me to "get over" things. They gave me time to grieve. Feeling painful emotions is not a bad thing. I learned it is part of the healing process. The church was, and continues to be, my greatest support system.

I remember my therapist asking me if I was angry with God after Michael's death. At the time, I wasn't—at least I thought I wasn't. The deeper I examined my own heart, I realized I was angry. God, the sovereign king of the universe, had the power to save Michael's life and he didn't. For that, I was angry. I don't claim to understand why God moves (and doesn't move) the way he does, but I do know he is a good God, and I can trust him. Ultimately, it was this truth and the community of believers who rallied around me that ushered me into a healing place of peace.

Lastly, I learned to reframe my circumstances and find meaning in the loss when I began to help others. Since losing Michael, I have become passionately involved in suicide prevention. Advocacy fostered post traumatic growth for me. Pastors began calling me asking if I would speak with people in their church struggling with mental illness. I decided if I really wanted to help others, I needed more education. I went back to school and earned a PhD in Professional Counseling. Today, I am a Licensed Professional Counselor and I teach master's level counseling courses. If I can help just one person to find hope, then Michael's death was not meaningless.

The Bible tells us in 2 Corinthians, "Blessed be the God and Father of our Lord Jesus Christ, the Father of mercies and God of all comfort, 4 who comforts us in all our affliction, so that we may be able to comfort those who are in any affliction, with the comfort with which we ourselves are comforted by God." (2 Corinthians 1:3–4, NASB). When we use our pain to help others, our traumatic circumstance—our loved one's death—is not in vain. By helping others, our focus shifts from our own pain and allows us to acknowledge the hurts of others. Amazingly, this deepens our own healing.

Grace, another survivor, tells how she longs to use her hurts to encourage others. "I think that we have to look for the good and not focus just on the bad. Who knows? Maybe one day I will be able to share my experience to help someone else. I hope I have become more understanding and empathetic of people and their family members who are suffering from mental illness. Mental illness not only affects the person who has the illness, but other family members."[2] Recognizing that her experience with suicide bereavement has the potential to help others has helped Grace to process her own loss.

I am surprised by the number of people touched by mental illness who call me for help. What amazes me is that they call, even though our story did not have a happy ending. When people are hurting, they want to talk to others who have been there. They want to talk to a real person who is not afraid to be transparent. When Michael was sick, I longed to find someone with whom I could talk, who had walked in my shoes. It seemed there was no one. Today, I can be that person to others.

Even though Michael's life ended tragically, his story continues. After Michael died, I prayed, asking God to use his death even more than he used his life. It was a tall request because Michael's life was an amazing testimony during the years he was well. God is answering that prayer as people still call me, years after his death, sharing how his death has impacted them.

One lady told me she struggled with depression. She tried to self-medicate with illegal drugs, which only took her deeper into the darkness. She had decided to take her life. She went to church one final time to make amends with God before her death. She walked into the church and sat down. She noticed heavy hearts around her. She said the pastor began to talk about how this was not an ordinary Sunday because they had lost a dear brother in Christ. The pastor then proceeded to address Michael's suicide. This was the Sunday following Michael's death.

She told me that hearing Michael's story gave her hope. She was able to see a church that loved him and missed him. She saw the need for fellowship in her own life. She ended up giving her life to Christ and joining that church. She frequently reminds me, "Even though I never knew him, your husband saved my life." Even as I write, tears come to my eyes. God brought something beautiful out of something horrific.

CHAPTER SEVENTEEN

Since Michael died, I've done a lot of research on resiliency after suicide loss. One thing I learned is that we adapt best when we engage in the mundane tasks of daily living. I went back to work to provide for us. I had to cook. I continued to clean. I hired someone to cut our grass. I drove Jorjanne to preschool, and we both went to church just as we had before Michael died.

We need to make a conscious choice to maintain our pre-suicide habits post-suicide. As we continue to participate in daily activities, we learn to adapt to our circumstances and can move forward in the healing process.

Sleep is one of the greatest influencers on our mood, and in the wake of suicide loss, it can make or break us. One form of therapy focuses on maintaining a routine. Part of the routine is to go to bed the same time each night, eat meals at scheduled times, and to schedule downtime into our schedule. After Michael's death, I really wanted to pull the covers over my head and stay in bed. I couldn't because I had a young child who needed me. Being a parent forced me to maintain a routine, even when I didn't want to do so. Keeping a routine not only helped me, but Jorjanne as well. It helped to maintain a sense of normalcy in a very abnormal time.

Perhaps one of the most important elements of resiliency is resolving to get better. I was determined to move forward.

I told myself that I would get through this. I would not let this defeat me. While there is not much in life we can control, we do have authority over our attitudes. "The one thing you can't take away from me is the way I choose to respond to what you do to me. The last of one's freedoms is to choose one's attitude in any given circumstance."[1] We can choose to believe "I will be okay."

Sometimes we need to make a conscious choice not to allow the loss to defeat us. To determine that even though suicide is a part of our story, there are chapters yet to be written. We shouldn't allow the suicide losses in our life to define us. Rather, we should resolve to grow stronger and better despite these traumas.

If you are struggling to believe you can get better, try to imagine your life once you've experienced healing from the loss. How will you be different? Engage all your five senses. Where are you physically? Who is with you? What sounds do you hear and what sort of things do you see? Imagine you are in this moment of restoration. Dreaming of the future promotes hope; give yourself permission to dream. I know these steps helped me.

I remember closing my eyes and imagining myself at the beach with Jorjanne. I could hear the ocean and the seagulls as they flew over our heads. Jorjanne's laughter filled the air. I felt the cool breeze on my skin and the sand between my toes. The warmth of the sun on my skin felt soothing and comforting. I could smell and taste the salt in the air, reminding me I was alive. Imagining the scene slowly changed my focus from my present circumstances to hopes for a better future.

Lastly, our hope is in Christ. Our loved one's suicide did not surprise the Lord. I don't believe God caused it, but he allowed it. I don't know why God allowed it, but I do know he sees our pain, and he wants to meet us in it. He is the Great Healer and is able to deliver us from this heartache. Cling to what is true. God is a good God. He is still on the throne, and with his help, we will get through this.

CHAPTER EIGHTEEN

People generally mean well when they ask questions about suicide loss. Unfortunately, there are times the comments feel hurtful. Teresa told me, "There were other people who questioned everything, and they should have just kept their mouths closed. You know, just nosy. Wanting to know all the details and how did it happen? What did he do and all these things and where did you find him, and did you find him? All this stuff was so hurtful and so painful. You had to relive that every time you told the story and it's just because they're nosy."[1]

We have a natural curiosity, and when tragedy strikes, people long to make sense of the loss. Unfortunately, many people don't know where to draw the line and cross boundaries unintentionally. Some of the examples in this chapter may seem harsh, but they are true. Too often people feel pressured to say something, and inadvertently say the wrong thing. As survivors of suicide, we often isolate ourselves to avoid intruding questions whether intentional or not. We've already talked about the importance of relationships in the healing process, but we need to make sure they are healthy.

A lady told me a police officer pulled her over for no other reason than to ask her a question. He said, "Hey, so your husband killed himself? What's up with that?" Someone who should have been trained to know better.

Not everyone is safe. We need to know who we can trust, and who is just nosy.

The most cited hindrance to healing from suicidal loss is stigma. Some ask if you suspected this was coming. While the question may seem valid, it may increase a survivor's feelings of guilt. I know most people don't intentionally ask insensitive questions, but it doesn't change the hurt. Others didn't understand how this question affected me. Not only do we try to process our own feelings of guilt and shame, but we also must deal with the perceived blame from others. People asked all kinds of inappropriate questions, like what was wrong and why Michael "did it." At times, I felt like they believed their questions (which felt like meddling) were justified.

Strangers also add to the stigma. The invasive questions from others add to the survivor's stigma, leaving us feeling further ostracized. We feel the weight of the "scarlet letter" from the "S word" as inquiring minds searched for intimate answers to inappropriate questions. As survivors, we are already hurting from the loss of a loved one, and the actions of some individuals add to the shame, thus impeding adaptation and resilience.

Some people ask an unassuming question, "How did your husband die?" I have always hated this question. My first thought was, *you don't even know me, and it is none of your business.* Too often people asked me this in front of Jorjanne. Still today, when I tell people I lost my first husband to suicide, they look at me with pity and say, "I'm so sorry." Some mean well, but I feel like others are judging me.

During the funeral, a minister encouraged me to hold my head tall. He said, "Michael was a man of God. It was an illness that robbed us of an incredible man." His words encouraged me to resist feeling embarrassed. Because of Michael's relationship with Christ, we are assured he is now free from all the pain that tormented him on earth.

I needed to hear those words. I had felt humiliated and ashamed. After all, who would want to admit that her husband shot himself? I confess I still cringe sometimes when I know it will come up in conversation. Still, that pastor's words gave me the comfort and freedom to let go of the shame. Instead, I trust God to heal my brokenness. It is so important to remember a person's death does not negate his life. Suicide did not define the man Michael was.

It's been fourteen years since Michael died and two years since Sherrie passed away. At times, the feelings of shame and rejection return when I tell someone for the first time how they died. Feelings of blame. Do they wonder what is wrong with me that would cause my husband AND my mother-in-law to want to take their lives. I know these thoughts are unmerited, but I have had them, nonetheless.

One survivor wrote to me about the awkwardness of social situations. "One minute, everyone is joking and laughing and, the next minute, they ask you if you have any children," she recalled. "You tell them your son died, and they ask how. As soon as you say he completed suicide, the awkwardness begins. Things get quiet. They say they are sorry, and someone quickly changes the subject, leaving you feeling isolated and alone."

I struggled with my own feelings of guilt, how to deal with the perceived blame of others. The blame led to increased feelings of loneliness, and for some survivors it leads to broken relationships with the deceased's family and friends. Many survivors say as they worked through the blame of others, whether real or perceived, they experienced an increase in shame. Some have even told me about the desire to leave town to get away from the whispers and stares from others.

Blame acts as a barrier to adaptation; it impedes progress if we own the blame. Once survivors process and purge the blame, they then move forward in the healing process. The only way to eradicate the blame is to face it. While survivors often feel a need to protect both their and their loved one's reputation in the early stages of bereavement, freedom from negative labels occurs as we become more open about their struggles.

It seems strange, I know, but transparency appears to be the antidote for the harmful effects of stigma. By bringing the truth into the light, rumors are dispelled. Where I once felt compelled to uphold a certain image, now I feel a responsibility to be honest to help others. According to research many survivors find it therapeutic to tell their story for the sake of others; in doing so, survivors can reframe their own experience.[1]

Kristen started a blog about her grief journey. She remembers the day she unveiled to the world that her husband's death was due to suicide.

> I remember writing a blogpost and I called it "The S Word." It was the day I announced to the public world the manner in which he died. Up until then I just said, "My husband died." I never said how, but the people in my inner circle knew. I admitted that it was suicide and that was one of the most freeing days I had ever had, because on that day I was able to say, "This was not my fault."

Writing these words, being completely and vulnerably honest, freed Kristen from the bondage of guilt and blame in that moment.

Moving beyond secrets and shame into a place of transparency has the potential to kindle healing. I remember the relief I felt after telling my friend, Melody, about Michael's bipolar disorder—her compassionate response helped me to overcome the stigma I felt. We need to take personal responsibility for our own well-being and work to overcome the hindrances due to stigma. In doing so, we can shed the labels placed on us and see our story in a broader context. We can learn to find our new normal.

I learned we can't let shame or embarrassment keep us from seeking help. Despite my embarrassment over Michael's suicide, I knew I needed help. I leaned into the assistance my church provided. I had to humble myself and admit I couldn't do things on my own. The key is to refuse to give up. As we try to recover from the pain, we mustn't run from it. I had to give myself permission to feel the pain. Instead of hiding my emotions, I had to learn to face them with courage. We also must be willing to offer forgiveness where it is needed. I had to forgive myself for missed opportunities. If I could speak to others who are hurting, I would say, "Do not make rash decisions. Seek wise counsel. Live life one day at a time so you don't become overwhelmed. Allow God to carry you when you can no longer walk. Trust him with your tomorrow."

The prophet Isaiah wrote,

> Have you not known? Have you not heard? The Lord is the everlasting God, the Creator of the ends of the earth. He does not faint or grow weary; his understanding is unsearchable. He gives power to the faint, and to him who has no might he increases strength (Isaiah 40:28–29, ESV)

We may not understand why life is the way it is, but we can trust God to empower us in and through our sorrows. The passage ends with the assurance that:

> Those who hope in the LORD will renew their strength. They will soar on wings like eagles; they will run and not grow weary, they will walk and not be faint. (Isaiah 40:31, ESV)

May we find the strength to soar once again.

For a long time, whenever I thought of Michael, I could only feel intense pain. The pain seemed to ambush me. Months after Michael's death, I remember driving by an outlet mall where our youth group had once met. The building had been torn down and all that was left was a parking lot of rubble. I began to sob. This parking lot was like my life—what was once a place full of life was now left in a devastating heap.

It took time but, eventually, I was able to remember Michael with joy. I still have those sad moments, but now many of the memories carry with them happiness of a good life. Even now, as I reflect on the hard times, the pain is still there, but it is less intense. This did not happen overnight. Be patient with yourself and give yourself time to grieve. We will never forget those we have lost. They would want us to move forward in life and pursue happiness. Michael's last words to me encouraged me to plunge ahead and to make a new life for myself. At the time, I didn't want to hear that, but now I find comfort in his words. There is no shame in moving forward. Marrying Jeff was one of the best decisions I have made, and I did so confidently knowing it was both healthy and good.

I once heard a sermon comparing life to driving a car. When we drive, our eyes focus on the windshield, so we see what is ahead. We occasionally glance into our rearview mirror at what is behind us. If we begin to focus on the rearview mirror, on our past, we will crash. In the long-term, a perpetual focus on what was can prevent us from living now. While it is important to remember where we have been, we must focus on the present to get where we are going. I realize that losing Michael is part of my story, but it is not the whole story. Ultimately, there is a larger story at work—God's story.

This is evident in the life of Job. Satan came to God, asking for permission to test Job's sincerity. Once God granted permission, Job's life seemed to fall apart. He lost the people he loved most. However, God saw the complete picture. Job's vision was limited to the temporal. Perhaps Job would have responded differently had he known that he was being tested. However, God did not explain himself to Job, and he is under no obligation to explain his actions today. God is in control and has a purpose for suffering, even when he chooses not to reveal that purpose.

Why did God allow Michael to die? I don't know. What about Sherrie? Why didn't God prevent her death? I don't know. I do know that God is in control and that he wants me to be honest with him. God can handle our fluctuating emotions. He wants us to be real with him; he sees through the masks. Job was not afraid to question God. He fired question after question to God and was discouraged when he received no answer. When at long last God did answer, it was not the answer Job had expected—or wanted. I now realize that even if God explained to me why he allowed Michael and Sherrie to die, the answers would not erase my pain. Through the storm, I did not receive explanations, but I did receive the grace to face each new day.

Job acknowledged that he did not and could not know the all the purposes of God. He realized that he must trust God with his life and its issues. Job had been reminded that God cares. Job didn't receive answers, but he recognized God's presence in his suffering. Knowing God brings security, even without answers. The book of Job is an illustration of the truth found in Romans 8:28—all things work together for the good of those who love God and are called according to his purpose. This verse is often said as a platitude to those who are hurting, but God meant it as a promise. God may not always reveal his divine plan, but we can rest assured that he has one!

Not only does God have a plan, but he is also acutely aware of our grief. The Psalmist writes, "

You have taken account of my miseries; Put my tears in Your bottle. Are they not in Your book?"?" (Psalm 56:8 NASB). Because God is timeless, the tears of his children are always before his face. What an incredible thought! God never loses sight of the tears of his people. What tremendous compassion and gentleness the Father has to keep these tears in constant view. It didn't happen overnight for me, but eventually, joy did come in the morning. You can trust God to give you just enough light for the next step. He will guide you into tomorrow, one moment at a time.

CHAPTER NINETEEN

I learned that like others I didn't fully understand bipolar disorder. The highs and lows of bipolar disorder tend to be long lasting. The depressive and manic episodes of bipolar disorder are much more extreme than regular mood swings. Bipolar depression often lasts two weeks or more, while mania lasts a week or longer. As I reflect on the tumultuous times Michael and I shared, there are some things I wish I had done differently.

I became an enabler—codependent. When I returned e-mails and phone call or covered for him when he messed up, I prevented him from facing the natural consequences of his poor choices.

Yes, his bad decisions might have caused things to go from bad to worse. Michael may have lost his job, his friends, and perhaps even more. But falling might have caused him to get the help he needed. Maybe saved his life. I thought my world would come crashing down if he lost his job. Now, I know there are worse things.

I was consumed with fear. I was afraid Michael would lose his job, which would cause us to lose our home, and on and on my thoughts would race. Michael's manic episodes caused him to go on spending sprees that stretched us financially. I eventually opened my own account to pay bills, but I know he resented the money he earned was going into an account he couldn't control. He could have refused to give me the money and, in time, I think that might have happened.

If I could do things over, I would have gone back to work. Having my own income, our bills would have been paid, no worry about him overspending or losing his job. The additional money might have given me peace of mind.

A job would have also offered me an escape from the day-to-day highs and lows at home. Instead of dwelling on our problems, I could have focused my time and energy on something productive.

At the time, I thought working was not an option for me. I felt there was too much chaos in my life. In hindsight, that was the very reason I needed to work.

I believed maintaining a job would have been difficult because sometimes I needed to get away for a few days to collect my thoughts. At one point, I lived with my parents for a month to refocus. Volunteering might have been a viable alternative. I could have focused on others' needs, instead of just my own struggles. Later, I learned widows bereaved by suicide felt helping others was a protective factor—serving others has the potential to foster resilience in the wake of suicide loss.

Michael was ashamed of having bipolar disorder, and he didn't want anyone to know about it. I helped him keep it a secret. If we had been open about our struggles, friendships may not have been lost. Broken relationships might have been salvaged if people had understood why Michael was behaving the way he was. By keeping it quiet, we shouldered the weight of this burden alone. We needed others to come alongside us and support us, but they didn't even know we needed help.

Eventually, I did confide in a few people. Having someone listen and pray with me helped. Bringing our pain out of the darkness into the light was a major step in my recovery.

Unfortunately, the church can fall short regarding ministering to individuals with mental illness. Too often people with a diagnosed psychiatric condition are told they are demon possessed or being punished by God for sin. We visited a church with a friend, and during the invitation, an altar counselor who had been told of Michael's struggles with depression walked up to us. He began praying over Michael and then turned to Michael and said, "You need to get right with God. If your relationship with him is right, the hurt and pain will go away." I was livid! Not only was the statement bad theology, but it only served to "beat Michael while he was down."

A friend told me there is no way to live life without remorse. While I didn't share it openly with my friend, I was inwardly berating myself for missing a major warning sign with Michael. He said, "You can continuously beat yourself up with regrets, but the truth is you didn't know what would happen." That is so true. As I look back on my decisions, now I do so to help others—not to beat myself up. I've done my share of that in the past.

About a week before Michael died, I walked into the office to tell him something when I caught a glimpse of what was on the computer screen. He tried to minimize the screen before I could see it, but he wasn't successful. Michael was reading an article about ways to complete suicide.

I asked him, "Michael, what are you doing? Are you thinking about suicide?"

He answered, "No. I'm just researching bipolar disorder, and I found an article about the risk of suicide for people with the disorder." Satisfied, I'd left the room. Later, I hated myself for not demanding he talk with me more about what he was thinking.

For so long, I felt guilty over the anguish I felt. I was a Christian, and I was supposed to love God and others. Why was I consumed with so much rage? I thought I was disappointing God by feeling this way. I've learned that my emotions were normal. When Jesus was in the garden of Gethsemane, he cried out to God, pleading for help.

He knew that he was about to face the cross, and he was overcome with anguish. He didn't want to go there. He was perfect and sinless. His emotions were not sinful. The key is that Christ was obedient to the Father, even during intense, personal pain. It was not wrong for me to feel anger. I never used that anger as an excuse for me to do wrong. In fact, feeling angry was a normal part of the grieving process.

In everything, I see the hand of God. It was God's grace that kept our marriage intact. He carried me when I felt like I couldn't go on. Amid it all, I kept asking God, "Why me?" Now, I see God used this trial in my life as a means for me to encourage others.

As time has passed, I still ask the same question, "Why me?" Why would God choose to use me to minister to others? After all, our story ended in death. I am amazed how God has used the brokenness in my life to give me unfathomable strength. Suffering is a breeding ground for faith when we begin to recognize that God is at work, even in our struggles. Just as God had a purpose for Job's sufferings, ours were not in vain. Trusting in the sovereignty of God to work all things for good gave me incredible hope.

Thinking again on Jesus's time in Gethsemane, I realized that Jesus never asked the question, "Why?" He didn't ask because he already knew the answer. Jesus was facing the cross to atone for our sins. Even though he knew why he was suffering, he was still overcome with sorrow to the point of death. Knowing the reason behind his suffering did not negate his pain. We ask "why" because we are hoping for answers, but even with answers, the heartache remains.

Jesus responded to his pain by crying out to the Father. He fell to his knees and prayed, "My Father, if it be possible, let this cup pass from me; nevertheless, not as I will, but as you will" (Matthew 26:39, ESV). He was honest before the Lord about how he felt. Why should we be any different?

There is no doubt I loved the Lord before bipolar disorder entered our lives. However, I see now I loved God because of all he had done for me. As a result of our hardships, I have come to love God for who he is and not just for what he gives me. There were times when I felt like God had abandoned us. My prayers seemed to bounce off the ceiling. I faced a crisis of belief. Would I continue to trust a God who allowed pain that I didn't understand? Yet, trusting God was the only hope I had. Even though there were times I felt forsaken, I had to cling to the promises of his Word.

No suffering is pleasant at the time, but it has the power to benefit us by driving us to our knees in faith. I now see that suffering can be a blessing, albeit a painful one. James wrote in 5:11 (NASB), "We count those blessed who endured. You have heard of the endurance of Job and have seen the outcome of the Lord's dealings that the Lord is full of compassion and is merciful." God does not always numb the pain of suffering, but he suffers alongside us. Suffering demands endurance, but we do not face it alone.

CONCLUSION

If bipolar disorder had not touched my family intimately, my life would have taken a totally different path. Michael's suicide has helped to bring the horrors associated with mental illness out of the darkness and into the light. We hid Michael's disorder for years, but healing couldn't begin until it was brought into the light. Unfortunately, we waited until it was too late.

By sharing our story now, I want to bring mental illness and suicide out of the shadows. We need to talk about these things. There is still a stigma associated with mental illness. Those who knew Michael were shocked to learn he struggled with bipolar disorder because he was such an amazing man. His life and death are educating others about mental illness. His downward spiral with mental illness has shown suicide can affect people from all walks of life. Self-inflicted death isn't something that influences only the feeble and weak-minded. Michael was a high-functioning individual with a zeal for life. He was the last person on earth who I ever thought would die by suicide.

Losing Michael was like losing a part of me. By fighting to support others, I feel certain his death was not in vain. By sharing our story and helping to guide others toward recovery, I hope Michael's death will ultimately save lives. That is also my heartfelt prayer.

I have mentioned this before, but it bears repeating. The mode of death does not define a person's life or worth.

Sometimes suicide robs those left behind of all the happy memories because it becomes the focus. It is important for us to talk about the person who died and to remember them. There are various ways to honor their memory.

Some survivors create a Facebook page in memory of the person who died. Friends and family can write letters or post messages to the deceased. This can be a safe place to connect people who might be separated by distance, so they can grieve together and offer each other support.

Others have wristbands made in their loved one's memory. They wear them as a memorial to the person. When family and friends see others wearing the bands, they can find comfort in knowing their loved one has not been forgotten. Recently, the university where I teach hosted a Remembrance Ceremony where we released Chinese lanterns in memory of our loved ones who took their own lives.

On the one-year anniversary of Michael's death, friends planted a tree at our church in Michael's memory. We gathered and were encouraged as a minister shared his reflections of Michael. Jorjanne was baptized on the same day, making it even more symbolic for us. God had turned a day of grieving into a day of celebration of life. As we anticipated watching the tree grow, we prayed as a church we would also see Jorjanne grow in her relationship with Christ. The tree was a visual reminder of God's grace in our lives.

ABOUT THE AUTHOR

Natalie Ford is the Degree Coordinator for the Master of Arts in Professional Counseling and Associate Professor of Behavioral Science at Truett McConnell University. She is a licensed professional counselor and a certified professional counseling supervisor. For nearly a decade, she served as a missionary with the North American Mission Board. She is the coauthor of *Grace-Based Counseling: An Effective New Biblical Model.* Natalie speaks at numerous conferences and churches annually.

Having lost both her first husband, Michael, and her mother-in-law, Sherrie, to suicide, Natalie advocates for suicide prevention, intervention, and postvention services. Throughout the years, Natalie's message has inspired many to

- Dig into God's Word for messages of hope during times of suffering
- Rest in the sovereignty of God (God sees and hears you, and he has a plan)
- Trust God even when life doesn't make sense

- Take off the mask and risk vulnerability with someone trustworthy

Natalie has a Bachelor of Arts in political science from Mercer University, a Master of Arts in Religion from Reformed Theological Seminary, and a PhD in Professional Counseling from Liberty University.

She lives in northern Georgia with her husband, Jeff, where they co-lead a Survivors of Suicide (SOS) group. You can learn more about her at her website, www.tearstojoy.org.

APPENDIX A

BIPOLAR SYMPTOMS

Manic Episode	Depressive Episode.
Elated, Euphoric mood	Depressed mood
Irritability	Dysphoric mood
Grandiosity	Guilty feelings
Accelerating thinking (racing thoughts)	Inability to feel pleasure
Feelings of heightened concentration	Social withdrawal & loss of interest in pleasurable activities
Increased energy level	Suicidal thoughts
Decreased need for sleep	Poor concentration and memory
Erratic appetite	Indecision and slow thinking
Increased libido	Insomnia or hypersomnia
Grandiose delusions	Appetite changes
Hallucinations	Appetite changes
✧✧✧	✧✧✧

APPENDIX B

Warning Signs of Bipolar Disorder

One of the questions that plagued me was whether I missed the warning signs. I knew Michael was discouraged and distressed, but I had no idea how desperate he became. Unfortunately, some people long for relief from the pain, even to the point of death. Statistics show three-quarters of those who take their own lives do so while depressed. If depression leads many to consider suicide as a viable option, then we need to understand the signs and symptoms associated with the disorder.

All of us feel "down" or "blue" at times. These feelings come and go but are different from the signs of depression. If you have depressed mood, inability to feel pleasure, and at least three other symptoms from the list below, you need to see a professional for a consultation. If you are having thoughts of suicide, seek help immediately. The symptoms of major depression include:

- Persistent sadness, unhappiness, or irritability
- Lethargy or fatigue
- Loss of interest in previously enjoyable activities (anhedonia)
- Sudden change in appetite (more or less)
- Disruption of normal sleep patterns
- Feeling guilty or worthless

- Moving about more slowly and sluggishly, or feeling restless
- Difficulty concentrating
- Recurrent thoughts of suicide or death

What causes depression? There is no simple answer; depression can be multifaceted. We know our physical body is connected to our emotions and to our spiritual lives. When one area suffers, the others suffer as well. The simplest way to describe depression is as one of three things: circumstantial, physiological, or sinful. Treatment should vary depending on the causes of the disorder.

There are times circumstances are so overwhelming we fall into despair. Some argue this happened to Elijah when he took his eyes off God and placed them on his circumstances. When depression is circumstantial, we need to be willing to reach out to others for support. Counseling is especially helpful with circumstantial depression.

Other times, depression is due to physical sickness, such as thyroid issues, low levels of serotonin or norepinephrine, a side effect of other disorders, and more. It is important for anyone struggling with depression to see a physician for a physical to rule out any physiological causes. When the cause is biological, medication may be needed.

We do know medication is most effective for treating depression when coupled with individual counseling. If you decide to take medication, particularly an antidepressant, do not stop taking it suddenly. Taper off the dosage under a physician's guidance. Also note if you stop taking the medication prematurely, you are more likely to relapse into further depression in the future.

Lastly, when we sin, the Holy Spirit convicts us. When we fail to repent and change our ways, we may experience a form of depression. Jonah despaired of his life because of his hatred for the Ninevites. His sinful attitude contributed to his anguish and misery. When depression is spiritual, repentance is necessary for healing.

If you are depressed, ask yourself the following questions:

- Has anything happened in my life to contribute to my sadness?
- When was the last time I had a physical exam?
- Is there unconfessed sin in my life?

Studies show that very few people snap out of depression without treatment. The answers to these questions will help you to know what you need to do in order to combat the depression.

APPENDIX C

WARNING SIGNS OF SUICIDE

Sadly, suicidal thoughts can plague anyone, regardless of their background. Not everyone who attempts suicide has a mental illness, but many do. Not everyone who ponders suicide will try. While we cannot read someone else's mind, we need to keep our eyes open to clues that suggest someone is contemplating self-harm.

How can you tell if someone is thinking of killing himself? While there is no foolproof way to predict it, professionals point to the following signs that a person may be suicidal:

- Threatening to hurt or kill himself
- Looking for ways to kill himself, seeking access to pills, weapons, or other means
- Talking or writing about death, dying, or suicide
- Hopelessness
- Rage, anger, seeking revenge
- Acting recklessly or engaging in risky activities, seemingly without thinking
- Feeling trapped, like there is no way out
- Increasing alcohol or drug use
- Withdrawing from friends, family, or society
- Anxiety, agitation, inability to sleep or sleeping all the time

- Dramatic changes in mood
- No reason for living, no sense of purpose in life
- We need to be aware of these symptoms, in the hope of protecting those we love.

If you suspect someone is suicidal, there are two important questions to ask:

1. Are you thinking about how you would do it?
2. Have you thought about when you would do it?

If the answer to either of these questions is yes, professional help should be sought immediately.

Once you recognize help is needed, where can you turn? People want to be treated with dignity and respect. No one likes to be told what to do. When it comes to getting help, present the hurting person with options. This empowers the individual with the responsibility for his own recovery. The treatment needs to cater to the individual's needs.

Help is available in various forms. Some people may feel most comfortable seeing a family physician. This is a good starting point because the physician can draw blood work and do a physical to make sure the symptoms are not the side effect from a physical illness. Family physicians can prescribe medication. When necessary, they make referrals to a psychiatrist, particularly when the symptoms suggest a person may have mental illness.

Contrary to popular belief, psychiatrists are not doctors for "crazy people." When people make jokes about psychiatrists, it can be offensive to those with mental illness, and continues to promote stigma. Psychiatrists are medical doctors who specialize in treating mental disorders. They are well informed of pharmaceutical treatments, as well as alternative treatments specific to each mental disorder. Because they focus on psychological disorders, they are well-versed in the different medications and are better able to help you find the best medication with the fewest side effects.

For a long time, Michael sought treatment from our family physician. Our counselor finally convinced him to see a psychiatrist, and only then did he get a proper diagnosis. Due to their training, I highly recommend seeing a psychiatrist if the symptoms are long-lasting.

Some are not comfortable talking to their doctor but may be open to talking with a pastor. Not only does the person who is hurting need unconditional love and support during this difficult time, but his family and friends may need it as well. Pastors are often available to help. This may be especially helpful if you suspect the depression is related to unconfessed sin. A trusted pastor may pray for all involved and give encouragement from the Scriptures. Some churches or denominations have mental health ministries available.

Other caring professionals, such as clinical social workers, psychologists, and licensed counselors can also help someone who is struggling with a mental disorder or with a suicidal tendency. While they do not prescribe medication, they offer empathetic listening and therapy to equip the person with ways to cope. Michael and I saw a psychologist together, and she was instrumental in keeping our marriage intact. She taught us ways to better communicate with each other, especially when emotions ran high. She also helped Michael recognize his need to see his psychiatrist at times when he was spiraling downward.

Sherrie was also under the care of both a counselor and a psychiatrist at various points in her life. In her later years, she stopped going to counseling. Remember, medication works best when combined with psychotherapy. Counselors are able to teach skills to counter depression and are trained to watch for signs medications are no longer working or the person is no longer taking medications as prescribed.

Support groups are another avenue some people choose to assist them in recovery. By connecting with others who share similar struggles, people often find encouragement and hope. No one likes to feel desperate and alone. Support groups help people realize that they are not alone in their struggles.

By presenting your loved one with a variety of choices, they are empowered to take control of their own lives. If the person who is struggling is dissatisfied with the care offered from one source, other alternatives give hope help is out there. Some people get help from a combination of sources. With the abundant resources available, no one should suffer alone.

There are times when someone is a threat to themselves, and inpatient treatment may be the only alternative. This can be a scary time for the person receiving treatment, as well as for family and friends. I was not prepared for what I would see in a psychiatric hospital. I cried and cried after dropping Michael off there for the first time. Despite our fears, the care Michael received in the hospital was vital. He not only got treatment from a medication standpoint, but he was also educated regarding his illness. Likewise, Sherrie's time in the hospital enabled her to find the right balance of medications (bipolar disorder almost always requires multiple medications) and educated her about her disorder.

Not all mental hospitals are the same. Talk with your doctor. Ask others in the healthcare community. Some facilities not only medicate, but also approach the dilemma from a holistic perspective. One of the hospitals Michael stayed at would not involve the family in his care. A different hospital communicated with me on a regular basis (with Michael's permission) and involved me in the therapeutic process. Both mental illness and suicide attempts affect the whole family, so I believe treatment should involve the family when possible.

While Michael was in the hospital, he did not have to face the daily stressors of life (work, bills, family). He was able to focus on his illness and work with caring professionals on a recovery plan. Unfortunately, Michael did not stick with his plan. He didn't go to support groups like he intended, and ultimately, he quit taking his medications. Likewise, Sherrie failed to take her medications consistently, and began to self-medicate, abusing prescription drugs. Medication compliance is critical for recovery.

Statistics show that one out of seven severely depressed patients who have experienced inpatient treatment will go on to die by suicide. Suicides often occur as the depressed person begins to feel better. According to psychotherapist Richard Gillett, "In the depths of depression, they may decide to die and as the depression seems to lift they regain enough initiative to carry out the act." In fact, the highest suicide rate occurs during the six to eight months after the symptoms have begun to improve. Unfortunately, this proved true in Michael's life.

Family members and friends should know that the risk for suicide has not disappeared because the depression seems to be improving.

What causes a person to contemplate suicide? Stress and relationship problems are common for some. Others might be the presence or absence of certain medications. Look for patterns and see if you can identify potential triggers. Second, you need to recognize early warning signs. Is your loved one withdrawing from formerly pleasurable activities? Is there a change in sleeping habits or diet or withdrawal from social situations? All of these may be early warning signs. Counselors are trained in this area, and their expertise cannot be overstated.

How Can We Help?

There are also some practical things that can be done to help. One way is to develop and maintain a connection with the hurting person. People who attempt suicide are trying to end unbearable pain. The depressed person may feel alone and believe there is nowhere to turn for help. One of the major symptoms of depression is an increased sense of worthlessness. Someone who is depressed may negatively interpret the opinions of others. Consequently, we need to reassure our loved ones we care. We were created for relationships. When we don't connect with others, we feel empty. Now is a good time to stress their worth and value to you. Make sure they know how much they mean to you.

Another way to help is to assist those who are hurting in understanding and managing guilt. Many people feel guilty because they fail to live up to their own expectations. Depression causes a lot of doubt and isolation from loved ones and often causes people to have difficulties at work—if they are able to work at all. These factors can cause a person to feel great guilt and begin to tear away at self-worth. Guilt—not being able to forgive oneself—is a major factor in suicides today. Judas completed suicide for this very reason. He had betrayed the Son of God. What remorse must have seized him.

It is important to point out that guilt is not of God. The Holy Spirit brings conviction, but not guilt. Conviction leads a person to repentance and change, whereas guilt often paralyzes a person. It is very important to help those who are depressed to deal with their guilt, so they are not overwhelmed by its tremendous weight.

People with bipolar disorder may also need others to help them see themselves realistically. Negative or grandiose self-thoughts, depending on the mood, often skew their views. Do not let them believe the lies that stigma may have to say about them due to their illness. Remind them that they were created in the image of God, and they are deeply loved. Help them see they are valuable people with a disorder—the disorder does not define them.

Another strategy for helping depressed people is reminding them of biblical examples of people who battled between fear and hope. When Michael was down, we found comfort in the Psalms. David cried out to God from his heart on numerous occasions, and I found I could relate to him. For example, in Psalm 40, David wrote about his extended misery in the pit of destruction. "I waited patiently for the Lord; and He reached down to me and heard my cry. He brought me up out of the pit of destruction, out of the mud; And He set my feet on a rock, making my footsteps firm" (vv. 1–2 NASB). David's experience can offer hope to others who feel stuck in the pit of despair.

When depressed, people tend to isolate themselves. It is important those in deep depression are not allowed to remain alone. Contact with people who care is an essential aspect of their recovery. William Cowper was a poet who lived with depression as a steady companion all his life. There were times when his depression immobilized him, preventing him from even getting out of bed. He repeatedly attempted suicide. John Newton saw Cowper's tendency to withdraw, and he made it a priority to visit Cowper as much as he could. Newton stood by him through the repeated suicide attempts, even sacrificing at least one vacation so as not to leave Cowper alone. People tend to recover more often when they have a strong support system.

There are times when, in an attempt to protect their loved one's reputation, family members fail to seek help. They often fear their loved one will be embarrassed, and their reputation will be ruined if others know a suicide attempt has been made. When we are at our lowest, we need help the most. If the person has a heart attack, family and friends call for help without ever considering other options. Why is it when people with mental illness threaten to hurt themselves or others, we fail to call for help until the situation is dire? If we seek out help earlier, a crisis might be prevented.

Ever since Michael died, I have resolved not to let fear of someone being mad at me keep me from doing whatever I possibly can to protect them from harming themselves. You can deal with the fallout of emotions after the crisis has passed more easily if you know you did everything possible, because of love and compassion, to protect the other person. I don't want to live with chronic regrets.

One thing I've learned is the need to allow others to make mistakes. When Michael would come off his medication, I would nag and berate him for doing this to us again. I think it would have been more effective to find proactive ways to help him monitor himself. Creating a mood journal effectively helps many to monitor their progress. If Michael had tracked his moods while on and off medication, he would have been able to see the pattern of ups and downs for himself, without my nagging. Some people simply write down one word to describe their mood on a calendar as a way of tracking. Others use online software, such as www.moodtracker.com, to record their emotions online and the technology charts the changes in moods. Once he acknowledged his diagnosis, I expected Michael to follow his treatment plan perfectly. What I failed to recognize was Michael was not only mentally ill, but he was also human. He'd make mistakes. He needed my encouragement to keep fighting and striving for recovery. He didn't need me to point out his mistakes.

The key to getting help is hope. Fortunately, of all the psychiatric illnesses, depression is the most responsive to treatment. When properly treated, 80 to 90 percent of people with depression can be cured. Stop. Did you read that? It bears repeating. When properly treated, 80 to 90 percent of people with depression can be cured. This is wonderful news. There is hope. If depression is biologically based, "You can trust that God has some purpose in creating you with a physiology or biochemistry that is faulty and accept that as God's will for you."[1]

When someone is overcome with depression, they often feel as if life is spinning out of control. It helps to remember that God is in control, and his purposes are good and perfect. The depression is not without purpose. While the sufferer may not understand the reason for the hardships, some peace can be found in knowing God is in control.

Unfortunately, there are times when the best laid plans end in devastation; this was true for Sherrie. We saw the warning signs her depression was deepening. Jeff and his brother even planned an intervention to discuss options with her, but before they were able to meet with her, she overdosed and died. I cannot begin to tell of the guilt I felt. I am a professional; I am a fierce advocate for suicide prevention and teach seminars on how to prevent people from taking their own lives, and yet I couldn't save my mother-in-law. In the end, we are responsible to do our part to intervene and help. While we can influence others, we need to remember that ultimately, we can only control our own actions and not that of others.

APPENDIX D

HELPING YOUNG CHILDREN WITH LOSS

Children are resilient. What we tell children concerning death depends on their age. We need to be truthful with them but telling them the truth does not necessarily mean giving all the details at once. We need to allow them to ask questions and be willing to give answers. Often, we give too much information before a child is ready. Understanding death is a process for children; they will continue to grieve at different stages as they mature.

In the early stages, Jorjanne kept asking me when her daddy would come home. I'd try to explain he was in heaven, and he couldn't come home, but one day, we would see him again. After several weeks, her question changed to "Can we go visit Daddy?" Answering was difficult. "We can't go see Daddy, but we can write him a letter or sing him a song. Would you like to do that?" She didn't need a theological explanation; a simple response was sufficient.

I recommend using a children's book focused on grief to help with the conversation. One I found helpful is *Someone I Loved Died* by Christine H. Tangvald. Unfortunately, I didn't discover the book until Jorjanne was older. What I especially like is the book is interactive and allows you to insert the name of the person you lost and has sections for children to draw pictures related to the loss. Tangvald did an excellent job of explaining loss from a biblical worldview for children ages four through eight. Books on grief help normalize children's thoughts and feelings and are especially helpful when we don't know what to say. They can be read and reread to reinforce principles related to loss in a kid-friendly way.

A common fear for children who have lost a parent is the remaining parent will also die or leave them. Jorjanne needed to be reassured I didn't expect to die, but even if I did, her grandparents would care for her. Knowing took away the what-ifs and alleviated some of her fears. The key was for her to know she would be protected. Once I told her where she would live if something happened to me, she released her fear of me dying.

Here are a few suggestions for talking with children about grief.

- The most important thing is to be honest with our children.
- When it comes to talking with children about death, less is more. Resist the desire to overshare. Give them enough information to satisfy their curiosity, but not more than they can handle.
- Children need to know they can trust you. Avoiding their questions or lying to them can damage our relationship with our kids. I want to be able to look Jorjanne in the eye and tell her she can ask me anything and trust I will always give her an honest answer.

APPENDIX F

THE 4RS

The 4Rs are applicable to those affected by suicide but are designed to guide healing in those who are bereaved by suicide. In the wake of suicide, survivors need to identify healthy **R**elationships, learn to **R**eframe the loss, maintain a **R**outine, and **R**esolve to heal.

Relationships

We were created for relationships; we need each other. In order to heal from complicated loss, we need support from others.

Reframe

To move forward, we need to search for meaning. Is there anything we can learn from this? Can our loss help others?

Routine

Keeping a routine is essential for posttraumatic growth. When we do the things we did pre-suicide after the suicide, we slowly begin to discover a new normal.

Resolve

All the resilient survivors of suicide loss I've met share a common resolve to persevere. We must determine that if anything good can come from our loss, we will find it. We must resolve to press forward in spite of the pain, until we find healing and restoration.

APPENDIX G

Despite its efforts, the church has often fallen short in offering love and support to families and friends left behind after suicide. In the midst of grief, the church has, at times, been guilty of causing more heartache by suggesting suicide is an unforgiveable sin, punishable by an eternity in hell. This teaching is an old remnant of the early church, based partly on the belief that because suicide cannot be followed by confession, the sin is unforgiveable unless someone intercedes on behalf of the person who suicided. There aren't any Scriptures to support this view.

The Bible teaches in the Ten Commandments, "Thou shall not kill." Suicide is a breach of this commandment and is, therefore, a sin. The Scriptures teach we are only freed from sin through grace by faith in Jesus Christ. It does not suggest this applies to all sin—except for suicide. In fact, Jesus said that every sin will be forgiven, except for blasphemy against the Holy Spirit. This seems to suggest that a person's eternal destiny depends solely on their relationship with Christ, not on the way that they die.

I'm not suggesting God condones this behavior but, surely, if it were unforgiveable, the Scriptures would say so—and they do not. Theologian Karl Barth said, "If there is forgiveness of sins at all, there is surely forgiveness for suicide."

This should give great comfort to those who are left behind. I have no doubt that Michael is in heaven today because he trusted in Jesus Christ as his Lord and Savior. Michael's place in heaven was secured by the grace of Christ on the cross. The Bible teaches that nothing can snatch us out of God's hand once we have received eternal life. "Nothing" means exactly that—if we belong to Christ, not even suicide can separate us from his love and grace.

When most people think of suicides in the Bible, Judas is the first person who usually comes to mind. There are five other people who gave up? ended? their lives in the Old Testament: Abimelech, Samson, Saul, Zimri, and Ahithopel.

While the Scriptures seem sparse regarding suicide, they are full of examples of godly men and women who struggled with bouts of depression. Moses, Elijah, and Jeremiah all dealt with forms of depression. While their depressions were based on circumstances and were not due to a medical disorder, as far as we know, the feelings of despair were the same. Their recovery began when they recognized and submitted to God's sovereignty. When they were reminded that God was in control, they became hopeful.

While reading God's Word and trusting in his sovereignty may not alleviate the symptoms of depression, it can offer tremendous hope.

MOSES'S WILDERNESS JOURNEY

So often when trials attack our lives, we cry out in anguish and wonder where God is. We feel God has deserted us and no longer cares. At times in Moses's life, his relationship with God appeared to be nothing more than master-servant, with no tangible demonstration of God's presence with him. Numerous times, the Israelites cried out to Moses in the wilderness, asking where God was, and Moses, in turn, brought the same queries to God the Father. Like many of us, Moses felt overwhelmed and inadequate amid his circumstances.

When depression attacks Christians, the believer may face periods of unbelief. They may doubt God really cares and question all that has been taught about the character of God. Eighty percent of depressed patients express self-dislike and low self-esteem, much of which is related to a sense of failure to be the type of person they felt they ought to be. This is especially true of religious people, and this discontentment naturally leads to doubt and unbelief. This unbelief is normal. Moses, one of the great patriarchs, questioned God—yet look how God chose to use Moses, despite his unbelief. How did Moses deal with his unbelief? He took it to the Lord in prayer.

In Moses's story, God delivered the Israelites from captivity, yet they grumbled and complained because they were hungry for meat. Moses had heard enough, and he came before the Lord crying out for help. Moses knew his personal limitations, and he was frustrated. He had no meat to feed these people. What was he to do?

Moses was lonely, and his burden seemed too heavy to carry. He despaired to the point of death. He said, "So if You are going to deal with me this way, please kill me at once, if I have found favor in Your sight, and do not let me see my misery" (Numbers 11:15 NASB). Moses was tired and longed for deliverance, even if it meant death. Moses had experienced many supernatural things as God's servant. He was the leader of a nation; he even saw the glory of the Lord. How could someone so close to the Lord go through a period of depression?

Depression can be used to serve God's purposes. The periods of doubt in Moses's life ultimately strengthened his faith. God allowed the Israelites to wander in the wilderness for a purpose. He wanted to strengthen their faith and dependence on him. God could have sent them directly into the promised land without the desert experience, but he knew the Israelites would grow weak and apathetic. He wanted his children to cling to him. Sometimes, God allows suffering in our lives so we can learn trust him with all of life.

Moses was not only a God-follower, but also a leader for God's children. Yet, he struggled. In an ideal world, Christians would always know there is hope and know that they can turn to Christ. In reality, there are times when life seems so hopeless even Christians struggle to endure. Moses's response in prayer is a positive model for Christians to follow when they are overcome with despair. Despite his feelings, Moses knew hope would be found in the Father. God had proven faithful to Moses time and again. Moses needed to meditate on the character of God and on his mighty works. By remembering God's past faithfulness, Moses would find hope to trust God with his future.

ISOLATION: A LOOK AT ELIJAH

James wrote, "Elijah was a man" just like us (5:17). He faced the same problems as other people. In this case, Elijah had a problem with depression. His pride was shattered, and he became a broken and depressed man. Elijah received word that King Ahab wanted him dead. He learned he had twenty-four hours to leave Jezreel or be killed. Elijah fled into the desert wasteland. He had been faithful to serve the Lord and saw great miracles. He expected great things to happen because of his faithfulness and was appalled God would allow King Ahab and Jezebel to seek his life.

I can relate to this. Michael and I were serving God—we expected rewards and abundant life to be the result. We were shocked when bipolar disorder began to wreak havoc in our world. Surely, this could not be God's will for us. He had great things planned, because of our faithfulness. This disorder could not be part of his plan—or could it?

Elijah sent his servant away so he could be alone—typical behavior of someone experiencing depression. Depression causes people to isolate themselves. Satan uses feelings of inferiority and inadequacy to cause people to isolate and pull within, to have as little contact with others as possible. When someone rejects themself, they find it difficult to enjoy other people. People who are depressed view themselves and the world as tainted because of feelings of emptiness, the loss of energy, and the desire to give up.

Despite what the depressed person may communicate, the help of others is needed. Depressed people need the presence of those who care. Sometimes, Christians don't want to reveal their depression because they fear rejection. Research studies show that people with fewer close relationships, a smaller social network, and less supportive relationships are more likely to become depressed. Humans were created for relationships with both God and others. God created Eve because it was not good for man to be alone (Genesis 2:18). The same is true today. People need the support of others. The most important thing to do for someone struggling with bipolar disorder, humanly speaking, is to be there when they need you. By spending time with loved ones who are struggling, particularly with depression, they are reassured someone really cares.

Elijah fled to the desert and took refuge under the shade of a juniper tree and prayed for death. Elijah exhibited symptoms of depression, wishing for death, together with loss of appetite, an inability to manage, and excessive self-pity. He was unmoved by visitors—even a visit from God and visions. The most common spiritual symptom of depression is to pull away from God—to feel God is rejecting you. This sense of rejection is often a natural response to anger. When it's difficult to see God's purpose in suffering, we often demand God bring restoration, and if God does not, the tendency is to turn away from him.

Elijah was angry. After all, he had just shown the prophets the power of the one true God. He was once strong. Now he was weak, and as a result, he assumed God had deserted him.

Scripture teaches that Elijah not only ran for his life, but also he journeyed into the wilderness for a full day before he sat down beneath the juniper tree. Exhausted from his journey, Elijah begged for death. Extreme fatigue had undoubtedly overtaken him. When a person is exhausted physically, his mental clarity is blurred. It is imperative that people who struggle with depression do not neglect their physical and emotional needs. Elijah found much needed rest under the juniper tree.

"There is little doubt that some—perhaps many—of the spiritual and emotional and nervous problems, which servants of God face would be at least much improved by more adequate food, rest, and sleep," according to Vicar Tony Baker. Lack of sleep and poor nutrition will cause the depression to worsen.

Elijah's depression caused him to pray rashly, to complain, to be suicidal, and to react with many other sinful acts. Given his attitude, a divine rebuke was expected. The amazing thing is there was none. Elijah was not chastised for his weakness. God met him where he was and called him back to work. God's compassion was magnified in his response to Elijah's depression. God continued to use him, despite his emotional meltdown.

At long last, God sent an angel to Elijah—not once, but twice—and the angel told him to "Arise and eat." The most important reason for someone who is depressed to get out of bed is some energy, some activity, is important to help the person to recover. Getting out of bed is a major ordeal for those who are depressed. Elijah was so distraught, apart from the divine messenger, he would not have gotten up from his slumber, not even to eat. After Elijah rested and ate, he found both the physical and emotional strength to travel forty days and forty nights to Horeb.

Elijah was ready to give up. He had dealt with a conglomeration of fatigue, disappointment, anger, and sadness. But God didn't give up on Elijah. In a cave, the

Lord came to Elijah and encouraged him. Elijah complained he was the only faithful follower left. Elijah felt not only fear and despondency, but loneliness. God responded to him, "Yet I will leave seven thousand in Israel, all the knees that have not bowed to Baal and every mouth that has not kissed him" (I Kings 19:18 ESV). It is astounding to imagine Elijah knew none of the seven thousand people the Lord noted. Had he become so caught up in himself he failed to recognize the other believers around him?

Such self-absorption is another symptom of depression. People in the pit of depression often feel as if no one could possibly understand, much less care. Eventually, Elijah discovered he was not alone at all, and his comrades were more numerous than he imagined. The same is true for many who are depressed, but they fail to see the people in their lives who care because of the thick fog clouding their vision. Having a caring support system is a crucial element of recovery.

JEREMIAH'S BITTERNESS AND LOSS OF HOPE

Planning to serve as a priest, Jeremiah was called by God to be a prophet. He was to warn Jerusalem of the Lord's coming wrath. Jeremiah didn't anticipate that obedience to God would be accompanied with suffering. Jeremiah suffered greatly as he sought to fulfill this task. His lament was so great that he cursed the day he was born.

> Cursed be the day on which I was born! The day when my mother bore me, let it not be blessed! Cursed be the man who brought the news to my father, "A son is born to you," making him very glad. Let that man be like the cities that the LORD overthrew without pity; let him hear a cry in the morning and an alarm at noon, because he did not kill me in the womb; so my mother would have been my grave, and her womb forever great. Why did I come out from the womb to see toil and sorrow, and spend my days in shame? Jeremiah 20:14 -18 ESV.

Despite his despair, this same man later penned the words of 29:11: "'For I know the plans I have for you, declares the Lord, plans for welfare[a] and not for evil, to give you a future and a hope." (ESV). How could Jeremiah experience such utter despair and, later, such incredible hope—when nothing about his circumstances had changed? Why? Because behind the pain of human calamity is the faithful presence of God.

In Lamentations, a glimpse is given into the heart of Jeremiah. He felt as though life had assaulted him with bitterness and hardship. He felt forgotten. Jeremiah felt as though he was chained in some dungeon where God would not answer his cries for help. Many of Michael's journal entries reflect his feelings of abandonment. In the dark night of his soul, he, too, felt neglected by God. Like Jeremiah, Michael thought his sufferings were because he had been alienated from God's favor. How often are Christians told their depression is a result of displeasing God? Was this true in Jeremiah's case? Certainly not.

The "weeping prophet" is a perfect example of someone who was obedient to God and yet still suffered greatly. Jeremiah's experience shows us how difficult a life of discipleship and obedience to Christ can be. It also shows God's presence and grace in our darkest hours. When Jeremiah meditated on his circumstances, he grieved. In Lamentations, he cried, "So I say, "My strength has failed, and so has my hope from the Lord."" (3:18 NASB). When Jeremiah focused on his circumstances, all he felt was despair. In time, God spoke to Jeremiah, and his focus shifted from his present circumstances to the power of the Almighty. Nothing about his circumstances had changed—only his focus. Jeremiah ceased to dwell on his situation and began to trust God with the outcome.

Once Jeremiah's attention shifted from his current condition to God's promises, a remarkable transition seemed to take place in his attitude. Jeremiah realized the trustworthiness of God in the midst of his depression. Jeremiah was even thrown into a cistern to die, but no more complaints are recorded in the book of Jeremiah after chapter 20. God mightily used Jeremiah even during those dark days when Jeremiah wished he had never been born.

Just as Jeremiah had to shift his focus away from his circumstances, those struggling with depression need to turn their focus to the Lord. Focusing on the depression empowers it. Meditating on the sovereignty of God offers the sufferer hope. Jeremiah encourages us to trust God as we patiently endure the painful experiences that may come our way. By remembering how Jeremiah meditated on the unfailing love of God while feeling abandoned, oppressed, humiliated and bitter, those struggling with depression can find hope and encouragement during times of distress.

SPIRITUAL BLESSING: PSALM 73

Sometimes, depressed believers struggle to understand why God would allow the hopelessness of depression to overtake them, despite their faith. Depression can be a spiritual blessing, although an unpleasant one. How? Those times of darkness often force people to cry out to God. Millions are pleading with God to take away their pain, and at times, God refuses. How can those who are depressed find hope to endure? According to Paul, "tribulation brings about perseverance; and perseverance, proven character; and proven character, hope; and hope does not disappoint, because the love of God has been poured out within our hearts through the Holy Spirit" (Romans 5:3-5 NASB). God's sovereignty and his Word offer hope to believers who are affected by depression.

All of us must persevere in our own struggles to find intimacy with God. There is delight in holding a newborn baby, but it is incomparable to the joy a new mother feels after the travails of childbirth the first time her eyes rest on her new child. She feels a closeness and connection to the child because of the toils she faced to bring the baby into the world. In the same way, the sufferer will come to a greater understanding of who God is because of suffering. A.W. Tozer said this about pain and suffering:

> Slowly, you will discover God's love in your suffering. Your heart will begin to approve the whole thing. You will learn what all the schools in the world could not teach you—the healing action of faith without supporting pleasure. You will feel and understand the ministry of the night—its power to purify, to detach, to humble, to destroy the fear of death. ... You will learn that pain can sometimes do what even joy cannot, such as exposing the vanity of earth's trifles.[2]

In this respect, suffering can be a spiritual blessing. In Psalm 73, the writer's beliefs about God collided with his personal experience. He had been taught God is good to those who are pure in heart, yet he saw many wicked people who seemed to have no struggles and seemed to be blessed. He was a man with a pure heart. This man knew the Word and lived a life of obedience to God. He was a good man, but he was not equipped to cope with his illness. Like many of us, he wondered why he, who had endeavored to live a righteous life, suffered while the wicked enjoyed life. This outcome seems an injustice, and the psalmist was tempted to turn his back on all he had known and learned about God. Day after day, this vexed and plagued him, leaving him in a state of depression.

As the Psalmist wrestled with these apparent inconsistencies, he came to realize God was all he had. God was his strength and would never forsake him. As he recognized God's presence, the psalmist became assured of heavenly protection and guidance. Because of his time of suffering, the psalmist came to understand God's goodness in a significantly different sense. He came to know the Lord as his Refuge. All who turn to him will find him and experience the peace that comes from resting in his presence.

Before Michael's struggle with bipolar disorder and his subsequent death, I loved God because of all he had given to me. Now I've learned to love him because of who he is and not because of what he has done for me. Much like the psalmist, my relationship with God was enriched and deepened because of the intense struggles I faced. In his illness, the Psalmist thought he had been abandoned by God, but he later realized he had never been alone. I, too, have come to experience this precious gift: the presence of God.

If suffering drives a person to God, is it necessarily a bad thing? No doubt, it is not pleasant. Yet, if it allows its bearer to experience the depths of God's love in a deeper and more meaningful way, it is possible that a blessing is part of the plan. We exercise to build muscle. In the same sense, our heavenly Father may permit his children to struggle to build our spiritual strength.

Christians are not immune to the struggles of this world; C.S. Lewis referred to pain as "God's megaphone." Allowing suffering in our lives is a fail-safe way for God to get our attention. In times of pain and heartache, we tend to cry out to him. When we are weak, he is made strong. Indeed, his strength covers any pain we may endure. Suffering does not have to be in vain. God can, and often does, use our weaknesses. Moses questioned God. Elijah withdrew from society and hoped to die. Jeremiah was depressed and suicidal. The psalmist longed for easier days. Knowing that God has redeemed my pain somehow makes it more bearable. The sting has become less harrowing.

Be encouraged, my friend; no matter how challenging the struggle, God's grace is sufficient. Romans 12:12 commands us to rejoice in hope, be patient in tribulation, and be constant in prayer. When hope seems impossible to attain, pray, and ask God to restore your hope. Cling to what you know is true.

God is a good God. He is still on the throne. We can trust him.

RECOMMENDED READING

Biebel, David & Foster, Suzanne. *Finding Your Way after the Suicide of Someone You Love*. Grand Rapids: Zondervan. 2005.

Fast, Julie A. & Preston, John D. *Loving Someone with Bipolar Disorder: Understanding and Helping Your Partner*. Oakland, CA: New Harbinger. 2012.

Hsu, Albert. *Grieving a Suicide: A Loved One's Search for Comfort, Answers, and Hope*. Downers Grove: Intervarsity Press. 2017.

Myers, Michael & Fine, Carla. *Touched by Suicide: Hope and Healing After Loss*. New York: Avery. 2006.

Omartian, Stormie. *Just Enough Light for the Step I'm On*. Eugene, Oregon: Harvest House. 1999.

Rosen, Laura Epstein. *When Someone You Love is Depressed: How to Help Your Loved One Without Losing Yourself*. New York: The Free Press. 1996.

Schulte, Rita A. *Surviving Suicide Loss: Making Your Way Beyond the Ruins*. Chicago: Moody Press. 2021.

FOR CHILDREN

Alcorn, Randy and Linda Washington. *Heaven for Kids*. Carol Stream: Tyndale. 2006.

Alcorn, Randy. *Tell Me about Heaven*. Wheaton: Crossway. 2007.

Sesame Street. *When Families Grieve* Kit. Sesame Street Talk Listen Connect. 2010.

Tangvald, Christine Harder. *Someone I Loved Died.* Colorado Springs: David C. Cook Publishing. 2018.

Wyland, Donna and Davis, Lynn Marie. *Your Home in Heaven.* Plymouth, Massachusetts: Elk Lake Publishing, Inc. 2020.

Wyland, Donna and Davis, Lynn Marie. *Your Home in Heaven-Curriculum.* Plymouth, Massachusetts: Elk Lake Publishing, Inc. 2021.

ENDNOTES

INTRODUCTION
1. Jeremiah 29:11–14.

CHAPTER 14
1. John 11:35.

CHAPTER 15
1. Romans 8:28.
2. Viktor Frankl, *Man's Search for Meaning*. (Boston, MA: Beacon Press, 2006), 135.

CHAPTER 16
1. Jonah 4:8.
2. Natalie Ford, *Resiliency Among Widows Who Lost Their Husbands to Suicide: An Interpretative Phenomenological Analysis*. (doctoral dissertation, 2016), 127.
3. 2 Corinthians 1:3-4
4. Ford, *Resiliency Among Widows Who Lost Their Husbands to Suicide: An Interpretative Phenomenological Analysis*. (doctoral dissertation, 2016), 132

CHAPTER 17
1. Viktor Frankl, *Man's Search for Meaning*. (Boston, MA: Beacon Press, 2006).

CHAPTER 18
1. Kari Madeleine Dyregrov, Gudrun Dieserud, Heidi Marie Hjelmeland, Melanie Straiton, Mette Lyberg Rasmussen,

Birthe Loa Knizek, & Antoon Adrian Leenaars. "Meaning-making through Psychological Autopsy Interviews: The Value of Participating in Qualitative Research for those Bereaved by Suicide." in *Death Studies*, 35(8), (2011), 685–710. Retrieved from http://dx.doi.org/10.1080/07481187.2011.553310

2. Kari Madeleine Dyregrov, Gudrun Dieserud, Heidi Marie Hjelmeland, Melanie Straiton, Mette Lyberg Rasmussen, Birthe Loa Knizek, & Antoon Adrian Leenaars. "Meaning-making through psychological autopsy interviews: The value of participating in qualitative research for those bereaved by suicide." in Death Studies, 35(8), (2011), 685-710. Retrieved from http://dx.doi.org/10.1080/07481187.2011.553310

3. Natalie Ford, Resiliency Among Widows Who Lost Their Husbands to Suicide: An Interpretative Phenomenological Analysis. (A doctoral dissertation, 2016), 148.

4. Isaiah 40:28-29.

5. Isaiah 40:31

6. Psalm 56:8.

CHAPTER 19

1. Matthew 26:39.

APPENDIX C

1. Natalie Ford, *Resiliency Among Widows Who Lost Their Husbands to Suicide: An Interpretative Phenomenological Analysis.* (doctoral dissertation, 2016), 127.

APPENDIX G

1. Tony Baker, "Elijah—A God Just Like His," *Evangel*, Spring 2002.

2. A.W. Tozer, *Tozer on the Son of God: A 365-Day Devotional*, (Chicago: Moody Publishers, 2020).

REFERENCES

Dyregrov, K., Dieserud, G., Hjelmeland, H., Straiton, M., Rasmussen, M., Knizek, B., & Leenaars, A. 2011. "Meaning-making through psychological autopsy interviews: The value of participating in qualitative research for those bereaved by suicide." *Death Studies*, 35(8), 685-710. http://dx.doi.org/10.1080/07481187.2011.553310.

Ford, N., "Resiliency among widows who lost their husbands to suicide: An interpretative phenomenological analysis." (doctoral dissertations and projects. 1229). 2016. https://digitalcommons.liberty.edu/doctoral/1229

Frankl, Victor. 2006. *Man's Search for Meaning*. Boston, MA: Beacon Press.

RECOMMENDED READING

Biebel, David & Foster, Suzanne. *Finding Your Way after the Suicide of Someone You Love*. Grand Rapids: Zondervan. 2005.

Fast, Julie A. & Preston, John D. *Loving Someone with Bipolar Disorder: Understanding and Helping Your Partner*. Oakland, CA: New Harbinger. 2012.

Hsu, Albert. *Grieving a Suicide: A Loved One's Search for Comfort, Answers, and Hope*. Downers Grove: Intervarsity Press. 2017.

Myers, Michael & Fine, Carla. *Touched by Suicide: Hope and Healing After Loss*. New York: Avery. 2006.

Omartian, Stormie. *Just Enough Light for the Step I'm On*. Eugene, Oregon: Harvest House. 1999.

Rosen, Laura Epstein. *When Someone You Love is Depressed: How to Help Your Loved One Without Losing Yourself*. New York: The Free Press. 1996.

Schulte, Rita A. *Surviving Suicide Loss: Making Your Way Beyond the Ruins*. Chicago: Moody Press. 2021.

FOR CHILDREN

Alcorn, Randy and Linda Washington. *Heaven for Kids*. Carol Stream: Tyndale. 2006.

Alcorn, Randy. *Tell Me about Heaven*. Wheaton: Crossway. 2007.

Sesame Street. *When Families Grieve* Kit. Sesame Street Talk Listen Connect. 2010.

Tangvald, Christine Harder. *Someone I Loved Died.* Colorado Springs: David C. Cook Publishing. 2018.

Wyland, Donna and Davis, Lynn Marie. *Your Home in Heaven.* Plymouth, Massachusetts: Elk Lake Publishing, Inc. 2020.

Wyland, Donna and Davis, Lynn Marie. *Your Home in Heaven-Curriculum.* Plymouth, Massachusetts: Elk Lake Publishing, Inc. 2021.

Made in the USA
Coppell, TX
24 August 2022